Anthony Peake is a graduate of the University of Warwick and studied at postgraduate level at the London School of Economics and The University of Westminster. He is rapidly developing a reputation as one of the world's most original thinkers in the study of altered states of consciousness. His work focuses on finding scientifically based answers to the great mysteries of human consciousness. He is the bestselling author of a number of books, including *The Infinite Mindfield* and *Opening the Doors of Perception*. See the author's website, http://www.anthonypeake.com, for further information.

THE HIDDEN UNIVERSE

AN INVESTIGATION INTO NON-HUMAN INTELLIGENCES

ANTHONY PEAKE

WATKINS
1893

This edition first published in the UK and USA in 2019 by
Watkins, an imprint of Watkins Media Limited

Unit 11, Shepperton House
89-93 Shepperton Road
London N1 3DF

enquiries@watkinspublishing.com

Design and typography copyright © Watkins Media Limited 2019

Text copyright © Anthony Peake 2019

4 5 6 7 8 9 10

Project management by whitefox

Printed and bound in the United Kingdom by TJ Books Ltd

A CIP record for this book is available from the British Library

ISBN: 978-1-78678-280-9

www.watkinspublishing.com

In memory of
Margaret Mary Frances Peake
(1924–2018)

CONTENTS

INTRODUCTION

This book is my fourth for Watkins Publishing. I consider these four books to be a reflection of my ongoing enquiry into the true nature of reality and the role of self-aware consciousness in that reality. Each of the previous books has taken a single topic and discussed it in the light of modern scientific research and the mysterious nature of anomalous human experiences.

The adventure began with *The Out-of-Body Experience: The History and Science of Astral Travel*, published in 2011. This was inspired by an extraordinary experience that took place the previous year. I had been contacted by the Swiss near-death experience researcher Evelyn Valarino. She was very keen for me to meet with two Austrian friends of hers, psychologist Dr Engelbert Winkler and neurologist Dr Dirk Proeckl. She explained that the two doctors had pooled resources and designed a machine that seemingly facilitated altered states of consciousness.

At that time I had written a series of books on altered states, and I was keen to explore the subject further. We arranged for us all to meet at Evelyn's home on the shores of Lake Geneva and for the Austrians to bring with them the prototype of what was to become known as the Hypnagogic Light Experience. What I experienced that weekend totally changed my understanding of what "reality" truly is. Through the effects of the Hypnagogic Light Experience (affectionately known as "Lucia"), I was introduced to a perceptual world beyond my everyday experience, a world that seems to be all around us even though in "ordinary" states of consciousness we simply do not perceive it. I was eager to know more. In my own writings I had explored the mysteries of the near-death experience (NDE) and had touched upon the out-of-body experience (OBE). But after my own powerful Lucia-facilitated perception, I wanted to know more about the OBE state.

In *The Out-of-Body Experience* I suggested a perceptual model of reality whereby human beings, and probably all conscious animals, exist in two states of awareness. There is the "waking state" – that is, the perceptual world shared by other consciousnesses and proven to be consistent and real by the simple fact that other consciousnesses seem to see, hear, touch and smell the same things. This is technically known as "consensual reality". The second state of awareness is dream perceptions. Technically known as "hallucinations", these, by definition, are perceived only by one person. Within this category can be placed natural dream states as well as perceptions facilitated by illness or by the consumption of psychedelics.

As is suggested by the title, the OBE state was my particular area of focus. This much-reported perception has consciousness perceiving consensual reality from a location other than the host body. For example, somebody might wake up in the middle of the night and find themselves looking down from a position near the ceiling. In many cases, the person reports that they see their own body from this location. Interestingly, a similar perception has been regularly reported during NDEs when, during close brushes with death (car crashes, cardiac arrests, strokes and the like), people describe watching the developing events from above the scene. Of course, these events can be explained by categorizing them simplistically as hallucinations. However, and this is a huge qualification, there have been many cases in which the experiencer has described observing events during the OBE/NDE state that subsequently were proven to have taken place. These cases are known as "veridical" OBEs/NDEs, and they suggest that the experiences are far more than merely subjective hallucinations.

An associated altered state is known as lucid dreaming. Here a person becomes self-aware whilst dreaming. In normal dreaming we perceive the dream environment but at no time are we aware of the fact that we are in a dream. We seem to simply accept, in our sleep, the bizarre and counterintuitive nature of dreams, lacking the self-referential awareness that we bring to consensual reality. However, lucid dreamers have a different experience. They know they are dreaming, and know exactly who they are. When this state of awareness is gained, the dreamer can manipulate the dream and can interact with people and other beings they appear to encounter. This particularly intrigued me because lucid dreamers regularly report that the dream entities they encounter in such states seem to show self-motivation and self-awareness. How can this be possible?

This made me realize that my consensual reality/hallucination model was much too simplistic. Reality, or at least the reality perceived by a self-referential consciousness, was far more complex. I needed to follow the rabbit further down the rabbit hole.

This I did in 2013 with the publication of *The Infinite Mindfield: The Quest to Find the Gateway to Higher Consciousness*. I was keen to know more about the experiences of those who, through natural or artificial means, accessed this world of dreams and hallucinations. I was particularly interested in a group of substances known as "entheogens". This is a fascinating word. It was first used by a group of botanists and scholars of mythology such as Richard Evans Schultes, R Gordon Wasson and Carl Ruck in 1979. The group felt that a previous term used to describe similar substances, "psychedelic", was inadequate. This word, coined by British psychiatrist Humphry Osmond in the mid-1950s, literally means "mind manifest". The suggestion here was that the altered states of perception experienced by individuals taking these substances were simply created by the mind. Ruck and his associates had come to believe that something far more complex was going on. They believed that these substances were giving access to another reality that is denied to us during normal, brain-facilitated perceptions. In effect, they override the brain's attenuation of the perceptual signals. The word "entheogen" was chosen to define such substances. It is derived from two words from ancient Greek: *éntheos*, literally "full of the god" or "possessed"; and *genésthai*, "to come into being". So an entheogen is a substance that facilitates the finding of the "god within".

Placed within the category of entheogens were substances such as mescaline, psilocybin, ibogaine and dimethyltryptamine (DMT).

Working on the book, I discovered that throughout history certain human beings could reach a state of "enthusiasm" *without* using entheogens. I have picked this word carefully. Enthusiasm also has its root the ancient Greek word *éntheos*. Enthusiastic dancing, drumming and various other rhythmic movements seem to open access to the "god within". Even in people not initiated in secret rites, entheogens could bypass the brain's inhibitory functions.

So by going in deeper into our perceptions, by looking inwards, we can find a whole new reality – or perhaps realities, plural.

But my next question was, what is the nature of these other realities, and why do only certain people access such altered states naturally? This resulted in my 2016 book *Opening the Doors of Perception: The Key to Cosmic Awareness*. Here I discussed the writings of Aldous Huxley, who suggested that the human brain, as I intimated above, acts as a barrier, allowing only a small amount of the information available to get through to consciousness. In his poem "London", 18th-century English poet William Blake coined the term "mind-forg'd manacles" to explain how we are trapped into perceiving reality in a certain way. But it was Blake's poem

The Marriage of Heaven and Hell that gave Huxley his
inspiration, specifically the lines:

> If the doors of perception were cleansed everything
> would appear to man as it is, Infinite. For man has
> closed himself up, till he sees all things thro' narrow
> chinks of his cavern.

It is from this that Huxley found the title of his hugely
influential 1954 book *The Doors of Perception*. Here Huxley
describes how his mind was opened by his encounter with the
entheogen mescaline. After this experience he was convinced
that consensual reality is but a tiny part of a much wider
universe, one that can be accessed only if the brain's attenuator,
or filter, can be overridden.

In this book I introduced what I called my "Huxleyian
spectrum". By this I mean that there is a spectrum within
which human beings gain greater and greater access to the
wider reality that surrounds consensual reality. I presented
evidence that people who experience classic migraine, temporal
lobe epilepsy, schizophrenia, autism, Alzheimer's and a
handful of other non-neurotypical "illnesses" have their doors
of perception opened, some more than others; and it is this
widened perceptual universe that brings about their seemingly
odd or irrational behaviours.

But at the same time I was struck by the mystery of the
entities encountered in altered states of consciousness. In all
the above books there are example after example of individuals,
either those on my spectrum, or others whose experiences are
facilitated by entheogens, encountering other intelligences.

I was also intrigued by the true nature of the environments
in which these contacts take place. To say that they are "mind-
created" fails to explain anything. We know from the latest
research in perception studies that everything we perceive is,
in a very real sense, "mind-created". The brain receives raw
data from the senses and converts this into a facsimile, and it is

this that is presented to consciousness. It is important to stress that this facsimile is not a one-to-one representation of what is really out there. It has been adapted and changed in many subtle ways.

As I stated earlier, we accept that the world encountered during waking life – consensual reality – is objectively real. We do this because other beings who share this environment see the same things and report back to us these consistencies. But what if a similar proof could be presented with regard to dream environments?

Over the years I have received many accounts from my readers describing encounters within dream environments suggesting that they have objective reality. One particularly striking case was described to me by Samantha Treasure, a London-based Canadian parapsychology researcher. Sam explained that when she was 15 years old, she was failing to concentrate during a school German class. The night before she had experienced a particularly vivid dream involving a white cat entering her bedroom and talking to her. When the class finished, Sam bumped into her best friend and they walked together to her next class. Sam related especially well to this friend because he, like herself, had had a series of strange experiences, and they regularly chatted about them. He asked her if she was OK:

> As we walked, I told him, "I can't stop thinking about my dream last night." He interrupted: "About a white cat."
>
> "How did you know that?"
>
> He smirked and continued, "And your sister let the cat in from the back yard because she thought it was your neighbour's cat."
>
> I just stared, shocked, as he continued. "And then the cat came up to your room and started talking to you."
>
> "How did you know all this?"
>
> His smile widened. "Because I was the white cat."[1]

This is an intriguing but not uncommon kind of incident. It suggests that two, or more, people can share the same dream environment from different vantage points. From this only one conclusion can be drawn: that these environments have an objective reality similar to, if not identical to, consensual reality. If this is the case, some intriguing implications follow. For example, if human consciousnesses can share the dream environment and report back to consensual reality on events that take place there, then what is the status of other, seemingly self-motivated, non-human entities that are encountered in this alternative reality?

That consensual reality is the only reality is an idea deeply rooted in the modern scientific worldview. But this is not how the universe is understood to be by all world religions and most esoteric and occult groups. For them, the universe is a far more complex place with many levels of reality. We exist in just one of those levels; and, in certain circumstances, we can access others. Not only that, but these other realities are home to numerous non-human entities, some of which are friendly toward human beings while others are hostile.

I first discovered just how real these non-human entities can be when I was contacted by American artist Myron Dyal. Myron had read my first book, *Is There Life After Death?: The Extraordinary Science of What Happens When We Die*, soon after it was published in 2006. He was intrigued by a concept I introduced in that book, something that has now become known as the Daemon-Eidolon Dyad. What I mean by this is a model of the mind whereby all human beings have two distinct foci of consciousness. One is the everyday self that exists within linear time and whose sensual world is firmly embedded within consensual reality. I call this the Eidolon. The Daemon, on the other hand, is, for want of a better term, the immortal self, the self that exists outside linear time and views the life of its Eidolonic partner from a reality that overlaps into this one, the portal between the two being the human brain. The Daemon has an awareness of the future denied to the Eidolon and uses this knowledge to guide its partner through life's challenges as best it can.

Myron contacted me because his Daemon, named Charon, had been very active in his life since a very young age. Moreover, on encountering my first book, Charon instructed Myron to open up communication with me.

Myron was born in 1944 into a God-fearing fundamentalist Christian family in the Los Angeles suburb of Inglewood. When he was four years old, he fell into a deep coma. He was unconscious for a number of days, and when he finally came to, all his previous infant memories had been wiped clean. He was reborn as a new person in a four-year-old body.

Whatever had brought about the coma also seemed to bring about a neurological change in the young Myron's brain. Henceforth, he regularly experienced intense epileptic seizures, which in turn brought powerful, deeply realistic hallucinations.

Myron became a very talented artist and musician and has long considered that his skills in these areas are directly related to his abilities to access a reality beyond this one. For Myron, entrance to this alternative reality is always facilitated by his pre-seizure aura state.

The first time this happened was one hot afternoon in May 1957, when Myron was around 13 years old. He had spent the day playing alone in stacks of newly mown grass in farmland near his home. As the sun began to set, the light became dappled, and this is when he entered an altered state of consciousness. Initially, this manifested as a golden aura that surrounded and engulfed him. Looking through the aura, he could see in the distance a small group of humanoid figures walking toward him. Out of nowhere a ball of fire appeared, struck him and then disappeared with a loud hissing sound. This made him lose consciousness for a second. When he opened his eyes, he realized he was no longer in a verdant Californian field but somewhere entirely different. He was in the middle of a vast desert plain with a ring of hills in the far distance. Surrounding him, he noted, was a group of beings wearing white robes tied with golden ropes around their waists. One of them announced to him: "Welcome to Zelcon."

A similar experience befell Myron one winter morning early in 1975. In the light of the rising sun, he went for a walk in his local park in El Segundo, California. In the dappled, mist-laden sunlight he spotted a movement near a tree. When his eyesight adjusted to the scene, he was astounded to see a small figure wearing a blue blazer and carrying a silver pocket watch. It was a white rabbit. He blinked again and the rabbit was gone. Its function seemed to be to switch his reality from one sensory world to another, because now in the place of the rabbit was a small leprechaun-type creature with a long white beard and a long-stemmed pipe. And in a woodland clearing nearby was a whole group of mythical creatures:

> Leprechauns, elves, white unicorns, all of them classical symbols of the elusive Trickster figure of folklore. Their numbers began to overwhelm my eyesight; I feared sensory overload.[2]

These creatures then faded from view and Myron found himself back in the everyday world.

Myron's hallucination fascinated me. What was taking place here? His aura state had seemingly shifted his perceptions in such a way that he was able to see all kinds of curious, indeed very odd creatures, all of which were non-human. The incident brings to mind Sam Treasure's dream encounter with the talking white cat that subsequently she discovered was a close friend of hers imposing himself into her dream environment.

I have long wanted to write a full-scale book about experiences of this nature. Many times in my previous books I have touched upon the subject of non-human intelligences. However, I have never, until now, focused on this subject as the main topic.

In this approach, once I had decided upon it, there lay a significant challenge. Non-human intelligences have been reported throughout history and across all cultures. It seems that we do not like the idea of being the only creatures who can communicate ideas, show emotions and create societies. We fear the unknown and have always imagined the world's dark places inhabited with entities driven by dark motivations. We have conjured gods and multiple levels of beings between us and them. We have given credence to spirits that inhabit the forests, the seas and the skies. It is important to stress at this point that although my whole approach may suggest that I accept the existence of these beings (and to a certain extent I do), I believe their existence to be "mind-created" – like all other phenomena accessible to human consciousness. Whether they objectively exist is a philosophical question I can raise but never fully answer: a full examination of the issue is beyond the scope of this enquiry.

The challenge for me, having decided on my theme, was how to structure my enquiry and how to narrate the story of humanity's encounters with non-human intelligences across history.

My first requirement was to find a collective term to define a huge number of diverse non-human intelligences. I eventually decided on the word **Egregorial**. In this regard I acknowledge the work of American occultist Mark Stavish, who defines an Egregore as an "occult autonomous psychic entity composed of and influencing the thoughts of a group of people."[3] As I shall discuss in more detail later, the word "Egregore" is Greek in origin and derived from *egregoros*, meaning "wakeful" or "watchful".

I also needed terms to define our everyday reality, the one we all share and consider to be truly "real", as well as the other place, not usually accessible to our physical senses, which the Egregorials themselves inhabit. For these realms I used two terms that have appeared in all my writings and will therefore not be strange to my regular readers. The everyday world I call the **Kenoma** and the hidden world I call the **Pleroma**. Again these terms, together with their provenance, will be further explained later.

Having defined my main terms, I then worked on devising my structure. My initial plan was to follow a strict chronological narrative. This would start with prehistory and work its way through to modern times. However, I quickly hit a problem. I was being far too ambitious in my enquiry. I did not have sufficient space and, I readily admit, the necessary knowledge, to embark on a series of discussions about non-Abrahamic religious cultures such as those found in China, India and the Far East. I decided after my review of prehistory to focus principally on the Mesopotamian civilizations, ancient Egypt, ancient Greece and then Judaism, Christianity and Islam. These cultures supplied me with a logical progression through time. The cross-fertilization of cultural memes could be followed through fairly easily. This worked well until I arrived at the Renaissance around 1400 CE. Until that time, religion tended to hold sway in the minds of most of humanity, with beliefs tending to be strictly controlled by the principal orthodox institutions. With few exceptions, heretical beliefs regarding non-human intelligences were not recorded; or, if they were, they were simply dismissed. But it was clear that the occult (literally "hidden") elements of the three major Abrahamic religions were cross-fertilizing at a level just below the surface, and these ideas erupted with energy during the centuries after the Renaissance and the Reformation.

At this point I realized that the chronological account could not be sustained further: I had to focus henceforth on the themes. The alchemists and magicians were working with esoteric forms of non-human intelligences, whereas the supposedly uneducated masses were encountering the inhabitants of fairyland, collectively known as the Secret Commonwealth.

With the coming of the Enlightenment and the Industrial Revolution, science started to take control, at least for the educated classes. Logic and rational thought were seen as the path on which humanity could progress. But in response to this growing sophistication came a similarly systematic approach to occult and mystic beliefs. Religion also reacted against the new rationality. Many of those nervous of change found comfort in the old ways.

The themes I have followed break down into the following groupings:

The Secret Commonwealth   This will be a review of the Egregorials that seem to share consensual reality with us and are identified as being fairies, elves, goblins and numerous entities that have historically been identified under the collective term "elemental spirits".

The Occult   This term relates to Egregorials that are evoked through magic (or "magick") in order to gain knowledge of or control over others.

Religious Egregorials   These are non-human entities that seem to disguise themselves within certain religious manifestations, such as angels or the Blessed Virgin Mary.

Egregorials of Mind Power   These are entities that are brought into existence within the Kenoma by the will of a group of human beings thinking collectively.

Spirits   Accessed by mediumship, these entities are usually considered to be the spirits of the dead, and may or may not have an existence independent of their creators. There is a close connection here with the Egregorials of Mind Power.

Extraterrestrials   In the 20th century, particularly after World War II, there was a marked sociological/anthropological change in the nature of the egregorial phenomenon. Incidents were often interpreted as encounters with beings from outer space rather than non-human inhabitants of Earth.

After formulating these groupings, I decided that the book needed a section that would approach the Egregorial phenomenon from a scientific perspective, specifically a neurological one. Hence, I have a chapter on those who seem naturally to be able to perceive Egregorials in their many forms, followed by a chapter on how psychedelic and other mind-altering substances seem to allow egregorial access to the mind in a direct way without the entities manifesting within consensual reality.

The final section of the book ends with a review of the relevant science and makes some tentative suggestions about what may be taking place in these mysterious encounters.

The Epilogue then pulls together what we have learned and suggests some pointers for future research.

As with all my previous books, I will take you on a journey across time and space. I will introduce supporting material from science and philosophy, and I will describe numerous encounters between human and non-human beings. At all times we need to approach the subject with a degree of objectivity, while at the same time acknowledging that just because an experience does not match our present understanding of how the universe works, that does not mean it never happened. Knowledge and understanding advance through anomalies, not confirmations. It is the "white crows" and "black swans" that push science forwards.

PROLOGUE

MY MOTHER AND DR JOHNSON

About ten years ago I received a phone call from my elderly mother. At that time she was in her early 80s. To give you some background, 15 years earlier she had lost her left eye after being diagnosed with malignant melanoma. She had accommodated this disability very well. She had lost her perception of depth but otherwise was fine. A few months before the phone call she had discovered she had glaucoma in her remaining eye.

This was not good news, as she lived alone, my father having died in the late 80s. However, she had rekindled a friendship with my father's sister, and regularly this aunt would stay at my mother's house in Bromborough Pool Village on the Wirral peninsula in northwest England.

In the phone call my mother described how she and my aunt were walking onto the village. My aunt had stopped for a second to catch her breath, and my mother stopped with her. As she did so, she noticed something odd in the sky over a local factory. She described it to me as a circle of smoke with a more solid, disc-shaped object in the middle. The object had two flashing coloured lights on it. She watched in amazement as the smoke ring began to spin, and then in a moment the whole thing just disappeared. She felt that whatever it was had, for a few seconds, been here and then returned to wherever it came from. Unfortunately, my aunt has even worse eyesight and saw nothing. My mother was keen to have my opinion on what she had seen. Although she knew about UFOs from my own interest in the subject, she had never read anything about them. I suggested that maybe the experience was related to her deteriorating eyesight. Possibly there was a "floater" on the surface of her eye.

A few days later she rang me again early one morning. Whereas she had been calm and matter-of-fact about her "sighting", her mood was totally different this time. She was extremely upset, and not a little frightened. Since my father's death she had lived alone and coped very well. Now something had occurred to disturb her feelings of safety. After I managed to calm her down, she told me what had happened. She had woken in the early hours of that morning. Her bedroom was illuminated from a street light outside her window. Something had disturbed her. She looked around the room and noticed the bedroom door was slightly ajar. She thought this strange, as usually she shut it. As she looked at the door, she noticed a movement. A set of long, thin fingers was coming around the door's edge. These were followed by a large head which poked itself into the room. The creature looked around and then spotted her in her bed. Obviously disturbed by her presence, it dodged back behind the door. My mother was, as she described it to me, petrified with fear. She could not move. She was trapped in this state for some time but eventually drifted off to sleep.

I asked her what her nocturnal visitor looked like. She said it was the height of a small child, with a huge, bulbous head. It had really long fingers and spindly arms. However, what really disturbed her were its large, black, insect-like eyes. She also added that it seemed to have no nose, just two slot-like nostrils and a pointed chin. She asked me what on earth it was.

I attempted to soothe her by explaining that it was simply a very vivid dream. This seemed to settle her mind. Thankfully, the "entity" never returned, at least not in that particular guise. But I was intrigued.

What can we make of this? An hallucination brought about by a brain that was showing the initial effects of dementia? If so, why such a bizarre and precise image? In his book *Supernatural* the popular alternative history author Graham Hancock describes his own experience with the psychoactive brew ayahuasca deep in the Peruvian Amazon. We will return to this substance in much greater detail later, but for now all we need to note is how Hancock describes the alien beings that suddenly appeared when the perception-altering effects of the ayahuasca took control of his mind. He describes them as being

> … quite small – three or four feet tall – but I'm only aware of their upper bodies from the waist up. I don't see their feet. Their white light faces glow like neon and are approximately heart-shaped with big domed foreheads and narrow pointed chins. Nostrils and mouths, if they have them at all, are just slits in their otherwise smooth features. Their eyes are completely black and apparently without pupils.[1]

How can it be that my mother, then a lady in her late 80s, encounters in what seems like a waking dream state a creature identical to two entities that imposed themselves upon Graham Hancock's ayahuasca-facilitated hallucination?

Does matter matter?

In 1773 the creator of the first English dictionary, Dr Samuel Johnson, was on a walking holiday in Scotland with his friend and biographer James Boswell. Their conversation focused on the idealistic thought of the Irish cleric Bishop Berkeley.

George Berkeley was the Bishop of Cloyne in Ireland. Between 1710 and 1713 he published two works, the *Treatise Concerning the Principles of Human Knowledge* (1710) and the *Three Dialogues between Hylas and Philonous* (1713). In these books he launched his detailed attack on the belief that material things are mind-independent. For Berkeley, everything that is perceived is mind-created and the external world is a form of illusion, or ongoing hallucination. Ordinary objects are simply *ideas* – which is why his philosophical model became known as Idealism.

As they walked along, Johnson suddenly kicked a stone, announcing loudly, "I refute it thus." To counter Berkeley, he was suggesting that the impact of his foot on the stone was sufficient to prove the solidity and reality of the external world. This famous gesture is now known by the Latin phrase, *agumentum ad lapidum* ("appeal to the stone"). Of course, this is nonsense. Johnson proved nothing other than his own lack of understanding of science. However, he did have an excuse: after all, people knew very little about the structure of matter in 1773. Those who still cling to this belief (I suspect this is the position of the vast majority of supposedly well-educated Westerners) are adherents of the belief system known as "materialist reductionism". Let's see why they are misguided.

Given that Johnson and Boswell were walking in the Hebrides, the rock Johnson kicked would have been, in all likelihood, a large piece of granite. So what is granite actually made of? Well, it is a mixture of two minerals: feldspar and quartz. Feldspar is made up of two elements, potassium and aluminium; while quartz is a mixture of silicon and oxygen.

The silicon atom contains 14 electrons, 14 protons and 14 neutrons. Oxygen has 8 of each; potassium has 19, 19 and 20; aluminium has 13, 13 and 14. That is *all* there is inside each atom. Indeed, each atom is 99^{13} per cent empty space. That is 99.9999999999996 per cent.

Let's look at this another way. Take, for example, the aluminium element of Johnson's stone. Each atom's nucleus, consisting of 14 protons and 14 neutrons, is approximately 100,000 times smaller than the atom itself. If the atom were blown up to the size of a sphere 1 kilometre in circumference, the nucleus would be a 1-centimetre sphere at the centre of the larger sphere. The rest of the kilometre sphere is filled with nothing other than the thirteen electrons.

Electrons are known as "point particles", in that they do not occupy any space. However much you could magnify an electron, it would always remain a point. So the electrons are not actually solid at all.

What about the neutrons and protons? Well, they *seem* to have volume and mass, but this is another illusion. The neutron and the proton are not "elementary particles", in that they are, in fact, made of smaller particles called quarks. These again are "point particles". So, at the basic level, the vanishingly small "solid bits" within the atom are not actually solid at all. So where did the atom go? Where did the molecules go and, ultimately, where did Johnson's seemingly solid stone go?

However, there is even more to the question than this. Johnson believed his boot actually made contact with the stone. But it didn't. At no time are we ever in surface-to-surface contact with anything in the external world. What we actually feel when we touch something is the electrostatic repulsion between objects, not the objects themselves.

So, Johnson felt that he had kicked a stone. But what was doing the feeling or, more importantly, what was doing the "refuting", as he so triumphantly announced? Remember, Johnson's brain is also made up of atoms which, again, are 99^{13} percent empty space. Put another way, if all the empty space in your body were eliminated you would be able fit into a particle of dust and the entire human species would fit into the volume of a sugar cube. This means that Johnson's brain is actually rather empty. And where in that brain can be found the consciousness that called itself Dr Samuel Johnson? Well, that is another issue we shall return to later in this book.

To turn now to a more general question, what exactly are the solid bits of material that make up the physical universe? With regard to our sugar-cube-sized mass of humanity, what is the true nature of this "material"? Well, it seems that even this "solidity" is not what it seems.

It was German physicist Max Born who, in 1926, first suggested that subatomic particles such as electrons do not exist as individual entities but are merely "statistics".

By this he meant that a scientist can calculate with great accuracy the behaviour of trillions of electrons but has no way of predicting the behaviour of any *single* electron. We only have a statistical chance of finding an electron in a particular place. Born termed this situation the "probability amplitude". He then proposed that the "wave function" of electrons is a statistical wave, similar to a crime wave. A crime wave itself has no actual existence. A person cannot be affected by a crime wave, but only by an actual crime taking place. Thus, the electron "wave" only becomes a solid, real electron when it is measured and found to be in a particular location. Before the measurement takes place, the electron does not exist except as a probability. The act of observation makes the wave function "collapse" into a solid object, in this case an electron. It is important that this concept is understood.

Before an observer detects the quantum particle, it does not exist. His or her consciousness brings the object into reality. Without conscious observation, there is no reality. In this way we create our own universe! (See pp189–191.)

In 1926 the wave-particle nature of electrons was suspected only because it explained the more bizarre behaviour of quantum particles. This solution has become known by two alternative titles: the Statistical Interpretation of Quantum Physics; and the better-known Copenhagen Interpretation. Named after the city that many of the followers of the famous Danish physicist Niels Bohr decamped to, the Copenhagen Interpretation was to give rise to a total schism in the world of particle physics.

Bohr and his associates were convinced they were correct in their startling conclusions about quantum particles. Not all scientists were persuaded. Albert Einstein and that other great scientist Erwin Schrödinger could not accept that there was not, underlying the quantum world, a reality in which logic and order were restored – a reality supported by what became known as "hidden variables".

However, experiments in recent years have proven beyond all doubt that electrons and even atoms do show schizophrenic behaviour. In the light of this, do atoms also come into existence as they are observed? If that is the case, you and I become much more important as inhabitants of our universe, because without us that universe would not exist. And do not forget, the brain that brings these atoms into existence consists of … atoms.

But what universe can this be? If the universe is brought about by my observations, it cannot be the same universe that you observe. I am "collapsing the wave functions" within my own realm of sensory perception. As such, I cannot be responsible for reality outside of my own senses. This idea is not new. The term "Phaneron" was coined by philosophers to define the unique world we each perceive. My Phaneron will, by its very nature, differ from your Phaneron. Taken to its logical conclusion, this means that every human being lives within his or her own Phaneron.

Thus, it seems that there is no objective, external, "numinous" world, and that the Kenoma is filled with nothing but mind-created images. It is indeed a "desert of the real", as Jean Baudrillard suggested.

The collective minds of all observing creatures collapse the various wave functions into a seemingly physical and material world. But this world is malleable. I would like to call this reality the Sensereal Realm. It is a domain that has its own borderlands, places where the inhabitants of the Pleroma can break through into the Kenoma. This liminal, boundary area was known as the *horos* by the Gnostics of antiquity. As I mentioned in my Introduction, I would like to call it the egregorial realm. I will argue in this book that independently motivated entities can use the minds of beings trapped within the Kenoma to manifest within that earthly dimension and, in doing so, fulfil their motivations. These entities I term Egregorials.

The question I attempt to answer in this book is a simple one: who, or what, are these entities? Where do they actually come from; and are they in fact real or just mind-created illusions?

As with all my books, I will take you, dear reader, on a long and detailed journey. I will not restrict in any way where our enquiry takes us. If the evidence points in one direction, that is the direction we shall follow. But we will always keep coming back to the main path.

As with all big journeys, we will start with a single step. And that step will take us deep into the history of our own species, back thousands of years to the start of human civilization. And what we discover there will, I am sure, surprise you.

PART ONE
PREQUELS

CHAPTER I
PREHISTORY

We know that modern human beings – that is, human beings with recognizably modern brains, like our own – have been around for more than 200,000 years. This means that our ancestors in the deep, unrecorded past had the same potential intelligence that we ourselves enjoy. It is probable that they soon learned to communicate using language, possibly even a form of language capable of abstract ideas.

The earliest attempt at communication was through cave paintings, the earliest of which have been dated at more than 40,000 years old. In this period, known as the Upper Paleolithic, paintings appeared in places as far apart as Western Europe and Indonesia. These earliest representations were hand stencils and simple geometric shapes. It was around 35,000 years ago that the first examples of figurative art emerged. Our ancestors were keen to depict animals and human figures. It is reasonable to conclude that this was a form of communication by which information could be carried forward to future generations. Of course, the information was rudimentary in the extreme. But it is clear also that symbolism and religious ideas are expressed in these images.

It is always extremely problematic when a modern mind attempts to interpret prehistoric cave paintings. But it is reasonable to conclude that these images also depict things that our ancestors actually saw in the environment around them. The earliest known piece of figurative art is a depiction of an animal found in a limestone cave in Borneo. The image is readily identifiable as a bull and has been dated as more than 40,000 years old.

However, there are some images that defy classification. For example, in 2018 an astonishing discovery was made in a cave in the Hoshangabad district of Chhattisgarh state in northern India. Hidden deep in the jungles of the Kanker region, about 130 kilometers (80 miles) from the city of Raipur, is a largely unexplored cave complex underneath the villages of Chandeli and Gotitola, containing a series of 10,000-year-old paintings. These depict curious animals, including what look like kangaroos and giraffes, which are not known to have ever existed here. So how, and indeed why, did the artists depict such creatures? Even stranger, however, are the depictions of human-fish hybrids, and humanoid figures descending from the sky wearing what seem like space suits.

The archaeologist leading the team, JR Bhagat, immediately noticed similarities between the entities depicted in these petroglyphs (cave pictures) and the modern stereotype of the alien. Another group of researchers discovered that villagers in the nearby Bastar region worshipped these paintings and, intriguingly, described how local legend claims they depicted small beings known as the "rohela people", who came down from the sky in spherical objects. What is even more significant with regard to our own enquiry is that the rohela sometimes abducted villagers and took them back to their own home in the sky.

In his book *Supernatural* (mentioned earlier in connection with my mother's "alien encounter"), Graham Hancock writes extensively about his own interpretation of what is being depicted in Late Paleolithic cave art. Hancock has built a reputation for himself as an enthusiastic promoter of the belief that humanity has a much more intriguing prehistory than that presented in the orthodox accounts. For much of the book he gives a fascinating but fairly conservative review of cave art from across the world. He analyses the cave paintings and notes that their images seem to be a mixture of entropic patterns (those facilitated by flashing or stroboscopic lights) and humanoid figures incorporating certain animal features. He calls these hybrids "therianthropes".

The real revelations come from a visit to a set of caves known as the Junction Shelter in the Didima Gorge, deep in Cathedral Peak Nature Reserve of the Drakensberg Mountains in South Africa.

Hancock spent some time in Junction Shelter, focusing on a particular wall painting known as the "bridge scene", which has long puzzled anthropologists. He noticed that one of the figures has a noticeable domed skull and narrow, pointed chin. This immediately reminded him of a very similar figure known as the "wounded man" on the walls of a cave named Pech Merle in southwest France, many thousands of miles to the north of the Drakensberg Mountains.

After escaping from an attack of bees in a cave in Junction Shelter, Hancock sits back and ruminates on these images of beings with such distinctive skulls and chins and realizes that they are a not uncommon feature of cave paintings in Europe:

> I discovered that more beings with the same combination of features, sometimes additionally with large, almond-shaped eyes, had been depicted in a number of other European caves. For example, four particularly menacing figures of this type, also "wounded", are engraved on the walls of the cave of Los Casares in Spain. ... research offers no explanation at this level of detail for such peculiar similarities in the facial features of supernatural beings represented by prehistoric peoples on different continents in different epochs.[1]

It is essential to realize that human neurology will not have changed in any way between the Upper Paleolithic and modern times, so any mind-altering substance would bring about exactly the same visions in both groups of human beings. All that could change would be the interpretation of these images.

During his cave encounter in the Junction Shelter, Hancock also made another association. The being with the domed skull and pointed chin reminded him of the entities he had encountered during his own ayahuasca session a few months earlier in South America.

The geographical, cultural and temporal spread of these experiences could not be much broader – an elderly lady on Merseyside in the UK; a middle-aged author in South America; an unknown artist from at least 10,000 years ago in southwest France; another artist of similar antiquity in the Drakensburg Mountains of South Africa; and a third artist of even greater antiquity in northern India, all of whom create out of their subconscious virtually identical entities. How could this be?

What links the five cave artists can only be supposed, but it is reasonable to conclude that all would have been involved in one way or another with the oldest known belief system of humanity: a tradition very generally known as "shamanism". It is to this intriguing and deeply significant approach to the structure of the universe that we now turn our attention.

Shamanism

Shamanism is an understanding of reality that seems to go back to the earliest days of civilization and is still practised in many traditional societies across the globe. Just because it is ancient and is found in less technologically advanced societies does not suggest that it is in any way primitive. It does not stem from lack of scientific knowledge but from a deeper, more intuitive mode of thinking. Remember that such societies are far closer to nature than we are, in our cities and in our technological cocoons. Supposedly "civilized" individuals rarely sleep under the stars or encounter nature in the raw. We are many steps away from an interface with alternative realities. But this does not mean that the shamanic model of understanding is any less valid than our own. I guarantee that any hardened materialist-reductionist person spending time with an indigenous culture whose relationship with the earth, and its associated "elementals", is shamanistic will have their worldview radically altered. In fact, we do not need to travel far within our own world to encounter powerful natural forces, be they psychologically based or externally real (and for me such a differentiation is a totally moot point). A night spent under the stars in an ancient burial ground or hours of darkness passed in a reputedly haunted location will draw up many atavistic and deep-rooted perceptions.

The word "shaman" is taken from the Tungus-Mongol noun *saman*, which means "one who knows". As we have already discussed, this general belief system occurs across the planet, but of course each culture gives it a different name. The reason that "shaman" became the umbrella term is simply that the first form of this system of understanding that Europeans encountered was the Tungus variation.

It is generally believed by anthropologists that shamanism is the core religion of all mankind and that all subsequent belief systems are simply adaptions of this core credo. By means of hallucinations, facilitated by various techniques or induced by personal neurological conditions, shamans were able to access other realms of reality and bring back information for the tribe or family unit. These techniques include rhythmic dancing to a regular and powerful drumbeat, spinning around, jumping up and down, and chanting. Some shamans can enter altered states of consciousness spontaneously, possibly through the channel of epileptic seizures or other neurological conditions. All of these methods allow the shaman to travel out of their body and perceive non-ordinary realities. This is known as the "shamanic journey".

The shamanic universe consists of three levels of non-ordinary reality. As I have implied, the terminology will differ from culture to culture, but in general these are known as the

Upper, Middle and Lower Worlds. Let's review these worlds in detail.

Our everyday world, which I have termed the Kenoma, is closely linked with the shamanic Middle World. This is where the shaman usually functions. In effect, this is Kant's noumenal universe, as discussed on page 38. It is important to realize that this realm is a non-ordinary counterpart of the Kenoma, a more malleable version of ordinary reality – what I term the "sensereal". This is the borderland between the Kenoma and the Pleroma, and it is the place where Egregorials can be encountered. As I will argue later, one does not need to be a shaman to enter this middle world, as it can easily overlap into the Kenoma during dream states, psychedelic experiences or neurological manipulations of brain functioning.

Shamanism considers that the Middle World can be very dangerous. It is not subject to human morality. The non-human intelligences encountered there may be, at best, ambivalent to humans encroaching upon their domain. Among the beings that inhabit the Middle World are the so-called "hidden folk". We will encounter these entities many times in this book: they are the fairies, elves, dwarves and elemental spirits that appear and disappear, seemingly at will, within the Kenoma.

Shamanism also believes that the Middle World is populated by the spirits of those who have not "crossed over" into higher realms of existence. What for me is of particular interest is that shamanism teaches also that most non-human entities encountered in the Middle World feed off the life force of living beings.

It seems that the Middle World is the easiest alternative realm to access for both shamanic initiates and non-shamans. It is simply the nearest non-ordinary reality to the Kenoma. The other two locations, the Higher and Lower Worlds, can also be accessed, but it seems that special sets of circumstances are required for a non-initiate to enter them.

The entrance to the Lower World is usually a cave or a tunnel that leads deep into the earth. The non-human entities encountered here are the spirits of nature – animals, trees and rocks as well as humanoid entities that are connected in some way to the earth itself. This suggests a journey inward, deep into the human subconscious, a place that Jungian archetypes and Plato's "Forms" can be encountered.

The Upper World is a place of light and seeming impermanence. It is a place of mystery, and entities encountered there are reported to be ethereal and fleeting. It seems that one of the major characteristics of a journey to the Upper World is that the shaman spends a good deal of time flying through clouds and encountering beautiful transparent beings who impart wisdom and advice. As we shall discover later, this seems to have many elements reported by modern-day out-of-body experiences (OBEs), near-death experiences (NDEs) and the possibly associated lucid dreaming experience.

Whilst in the Middle World, the shamanic journey usually takes a extremely macabre and disturbing twist. This is known as "dismemberment". It involves the shaman, usually on their first journey into the Middle World, encountering what is generally known as their "totem". This usually appears in the guise of an animal. It can be a small creature such as a rabbit or an owl, or a larger predator such as a wolf or a lion. At the same time, or soon afterwards, the "Teacher" will appear.

This will be a human-like entity, usually wearing a hooded cloak that obscures the face. This being will facilitate the brutal and horrific dismemberment of the initiate shaman's body. There are cultural variations, but in general the shaman's body is torn open, their entrails drawn out and their limbs chopped off. This may be done by the claws and teeth of an animal totem, such as a wolf or a tiger, or by the humanoid "guide" using weapons or surgical tools. This is all part of the initiation. Soon afterwards the body will be reassembled and the initiate becomes a practising shaman.

Romanian historian-philosopher Mircea Eliade was the first Western-educated researcher to analyse in depth the shamanic experience. In his hugely influential *Shamanism: Archaic Techniques of Ecstasy*, published in 1951, he describes the process of dismemberment and the shamanic journey that follows:

> The content of these first ecstatic experiences, although comparatively rich, always includes one or more of the following themes: dismemberment of the body, followed by a renewal of the internal organs or viscera; ascent to the sky and dialogue with the gods or spirits; descent to the underworld and conversations with spirits and the souls of dead shamans.[2]

Eliade is describing here specifically Siberian shamanism, and yet the macabre and disturbing element of the shamanic journey is found in virtually every shamanic culture across the planet and, one can reasonably assume, throughout history.

Also intriguing is how shamanic traditions from around the world all include encounters with the beings I call Egregorials. In this regard I would like to focus specifically on two shamanic cultures thousands of miles apart geographically: Aboriginal Australia and the tribes of the Colombian Amazon (with a brief interlude on North America).

Australian Aboriginal traditions

The indigenous peoples of Australia, particularly those located deep inland and in the north of the country, have traditions of shamanism that may go farther back into history than any other group. Their isolation has allowed us, through oral transmission, a glimpse of what our ancestors believed the universe to consist of.

In these communities it is believed that the most powerful shamans are initiated by non-human spirit entities known as the Iruntainia. These beings have their origins in the

Altjiringa, or Dreamtime. Significant for me is that the abode of the Iruntainia is always caves. Late at night the initiate shaman is left outside a cave known to be inhabited by the Iruntainia. He or she then goes to sleep outside the cave and is soon discovered by the Iruntainia, who immediately pierce the initiate's tongue, making a large hole which remains as evidence of initiation for the rest of the shaman's life. Indeed, this is the only visible evidence that remains, serving as proof that this person has been through the ordeal that follows.

After the piercing, the initiate is taken deep into the cave, where their body is opened up and their internal organs removed. In their body's cavity the Iruntainia place a number of magical quartz stones, known as "atnongara". These may also be placed in the initiate's arms or legs.

A second initiation process takes place a few years later. This time, another group of entities, known as the Oruncha, are responsible. These spirits are different from the Iruntainia: they are far more mischievous and they snatch the shaman from his or her normal life and take them underground. Soon afterwards, the final initiation takes place. This time the facilitators are fellow shamans known as the Nung-gara. Here a few of the original atnongara, placed in the initiate's body during their first encounter with the Iruntainia, are removed and relocated in different parts of the body.[3] We shall return to the significance of these crystals later.

In another Aboriginal tradition, the role of the Iruntainia is taken by another intriguing entity known as the Rainbow Serpent. In this process a snake, or a number of snakes, are placed deep inside the initiate's brain.

North American traditions

As I have mentioned, shamanism is a belief system found across the world. It has common themes threading through complex and diverse cultures that developed in isolation in different continents. Of course, in the distant past the ancestors of the

Native Americans had crossed Beringia, the land bridge linking Siberia with Alaska, and in doing so they probably brought with them many Siberian shamanic beliefs. Geologists believe that the land bridge was finally lost around 10,000 years ago. From this point of entry the migrants worked their way south and east, eventually populating both North and South America.

One of classic monographs on the shamanic traditions of the New World is William Beynon's *The First Nations of the Pacific North West*. Here Beynon tells of the Gitksan (Tsimshian) shaman Isaac Tens, who began his shamanic career when, in 1890, at the age of 30, he began to spontaneously lose consciousness. Tens was finishing a long afternoon of cutting wood in a forest when something strange happened:

> While I was cutting up the wood in lengths, it grew dark towards the evening. Before I had finished my last stack of wood. [*sic*] A loud noise broke out over me and a large owl appeared to me. The owl took hold of me, caught my face, and tried to lift me up. I lost consciousness. As soon as I came back to my senses I realized that I had fallen into the snow. My head was coated with ice, and some blood was running out of my mouth.[4]

Owls also appear in Upper Paleolithic cave paintings such as those in the Chauvet cave in southern France. As we have already seen (page 12), cave art seems to have direct links with non-human intelligences. Why did our ancestors focus on owls? On close inspection the Chauvet painting depicts the owl from behind but the head looks at us face on. This is one of the exceptional features of an owl: it can swivel its head up to 270 degrees. But for me the really significant point about an owl is the face itself. It is, unlike in most birds, fairly flat and the eyes look directly forward.

As we shall discover later, owl imagery does not merely reflect a fascination with something odd in nature, but may hide a far more sinister possibility, particularly for shamans.

The Kogi people and shamanism

In the mountains of the Sierra Nevada de Santa Marta in northern Columbia can be found the Kogi people, direct descendants of the pre-Columbian Tairona civilization. These tribes live in an area that is virtually undisturbed by the outside world, and this means that the Kogi can give us a fascinating insight into an ancient indigenous culture.

The Kogi have a profoundly shamanistic cosmology, comprising the underworld, the middle earth plane and the heavenly upper world. As we have seen, this tripartite partition of reality is a universal across all shamanic cultures. Why is this? Is it simply a natural extrapolation from the natural world, where the sky is above (subject to an upward gaze) and the earth is below (accessed through caves and potholes). Or does it suggest a deeper truth, linked to the way in which altered states of consciousness tend to present a threefold model of the universe? Are the shamans reporting simple observation or profound spiritual insight? We shall return to this question later.

Within the Kogi culture the shamans, known as *mamas*, are held in exceedingly high esteem. Shamans are selected at birth by divination, and once chosen are taken away to be brought up in total isolation, usually in a cave or other deep, dark place. For the first 18 years of their life, the trainee shaman, if they ever leave the cave, will be taken out only at night and with a full head covering. Thus, the child never sees any form of natural light. This isolation allows them to develop a special sense apparatus: their senses are trained to fully tune only into an alternative sensory world, known as Aluna. This is a realm that overlaps this world and the upper world. As things are believed to happen first in Aluna, the trainee *mama* acquires an ability to experience the future before it happens here in this world. Also, while in this state, the young shaman will encounter the inhabitants of Aluna, both human and non-human. They can live in this dark, isolated environment for 9 to 16 years before they are allowed out into the world of natural light as a fully developed *mama*.

Why is it that the trainee *mamas* have to be kept in the dark for years on end? There may be a crucial clue here about what is really taking place in egregorial encounters and altered states of consciousness. This is another important question to which we shall return later.

One of the main elements of shamanic beliefs is that they are, for the most part, oral traditions carried down from generation to generation by storytellers and by the shamans themselves. However, the invention of written language was revolutionary. It provided a tool whereby specific and detailed information could be transferred from group to group. Suddenly ideas could be communicated across both physical distance and through time itself. The discovery was made in Mesopotamia in the Middle East around 3100 BCE. Now egregorial encounters could be described in detail, rather than depicted upon cave walls. It is to these first fully fledged civilizations that we now turn our attention.

CHAPTER 2
ANCIENT
CIVILIZATIONS

Between 1983 and 1985 a number of curious statues and
busts were unearthed at the Ayn Ghazal archaeological site in
modern-day Jordan. It is now believed that they were created
in two periods, about 200 years apart; the general dating
is around 6500 BCE. The subjects depicted are humanoid
figures with large almond-shaped eyes, a tiny nose and a slit
for a mouth. Of particular interest to me is that the figures
are not of human size. The largest is around 1 metre (3 feet)
tall. They are also very flat, around 10 centimetres (just short
of 4 inches) in thickness. It is fairly clear from the limestone
plaster from which they have been moulded that this choice
of height was deliberate: they could easily have been crafted
to be the average human height but they were not. So what
are our distant ancestors trying to show here? Are these simply
crude depictions of everyday people of the time? If so, why are
their eyes so disproportionately large, why are the figures so
short and why is their skin colour whitish-grey? It is reasonable
to assume that the skin colour of inhabitants of the Middle
East, even so many centuries ago, would be similar to the skin
tones found today in Jordan. Some researchers have suggested
that the figures are of ghosts. But why should Middle Eastern
sculptures of 8,500 years ago correspond with the European,
19th–20th century image of a ghost being white?

It is usual for ancient cultures (and, indeed, modern ones)
to invest time and energy in depicting gods or other religious

figures. Is this what these strange humanoids are? Certainly they have an uncanny similarity with the creatures depicted on Upper Paleolithic cave walls across the world. As far as we know, written language was not available to the creators of these images, so we cannot expect to find out what they themselves believed they were showing. The same goes for the creators of the Ayn Ghazal figurines. However, curiously similar statues have been excavated in other, much later archaeological sites in the Middle East, and these *were* created by a people who had developed written language. So what do these voices from the deep past have to tell us about ancient egregorial encounters?

Ancient Sumer and Babylon

The oldest written records we have date back to around 4000 BCE and were found in the delta of the Tigris and Euphrates rivers in what is now Iraq. The civilization that reached this level of sophistication had as its capital the city of Sumer (the biblical Shinar). According to modern research, the Sumerians were additionally responsible for the discovery of brick making, early pharmacology, weights and measures, mathematics and astronomy. They seemed to have valued music and dance.

The Sumerian language was recorded in a form of writing known as "cuneiform". When finally translated, many clay tablets were found to have told incredible tales of human encounters with non-human entities. Indeed, the Sumerians themselves recorded that all their advances in civilization were facilitated directly by these entities. Collectively, these beings were known as "those who from heaven to earth came", which is covered by one word in the Sumerian language: Anunnaki.

The Enûma Eliš, the Babylonian creation myth written, it is believed, between 1900 and 1600 BCE, describes a great war in heaven resulting in the defeat of the Anunnaki and their subsequent banishment to the Underworld.[1] However, another group of Anunnaki, known as the Igigi, remain as gods of the Upper World. The Igigi are intriguing. According to the Hungarian psychiatrist Ede Frecska, the word Igigi translates from Akkadian into English as the "Watchers".[2] As we shall discover later, this concept of the Watchers is a theme found in many ancient civilizations and has become a bedrock of modern mystical and magical traditions.

What is significant here is that we have within Sumerian/Akkadian/Babylonian beliefs a cosmology virtually identical to that described by shamanic traditions from around the world. Although one could reasonably argue that such a tripartite model (Upper, Middle and Lower Worlds) reflects how things seem from an Earth-bound human perspective, this correspondence does not, in itself, undermine the possibility that such a cosmology has developed through actual experiences and that these realms do exist in the wider sensory reality.

It is clear from the ancient texts that the scribes of ancient Mesopotamia were aware of seemingly non-human entities that invaded the psychological lives of their fellow citizens. For example, in an ancient Sumerian poem we find the following lines:

The seven demons grip his thighs, They bite and tear his face, They slash at his body with an axe, They turn his face into the face of agony.

On a later clay tablet, discovered in the ruins of the Assyrian capital, Nineveh (and now housed in the British Museum, London), is the following narrative, etched in cuneiform:

… in the desert … they spare not … The ghoul, after man hath sprinkled. Spreading heart disease, heartache, sickness [and] disease over the city of the man, scorching the wanderer like the day, and filling him with bitterness; like a flood they gathered together [until] this man revolteth against himself. No food can he eat, no water can he drink, but with woe, each day is he sated.

It seems that the location of these three ancient civilizations, Mesopotamia, was a focus for non-human intervention, specifically involving sexual issues. The Sumerian goddess of love and fertility, Inanna, was known to have an insatiable lust for human beings and would sexually ravage the bodies of her victims, followed by vampirism and dismemberment. Her name derives from the Sumerian *nin-an-ak*, which translates as "Lady of Heaven". Her symbol was either an eight-pointed star or a rosette. On many of the seals that have come down to us from ancient Sumer, Inanna is shown with a star shining in the sky behind her.[3] This may be an association with the planet Venus, but it could equally suggest she was associated with lights in the sky. Her equivalent in Babylonia was the goddess Ishtar, who shares with her the symbol of the eight-pointed star.

There is another Sumerian set of demons known as the Maskim. This word means "ensnarers" – entities that capture and hold human beings against their will. As we shall discover, this idea of abduction is by no means restricted to ancient Mesopotamia.

In the late 7th century BCE the Assyrian Empire was overthrown by the Babylonians, who until that time constituted a province of the Empire. The Babylonian belief system, particularly with regard to egregorial entities, was virtually identical to that of the Assyrians, so political change brought no change of faith, with one possible important exception: in the texts of the late Babylonian period the Anunnaki had moved underground and become inhabitants of the dark places.

In 587 BCE, the Babylonian king Nebuchadnezzar destroyed the city walls of Jerusalem and fully incorporated the semi-independent client state of Judah into the Babylonian empire. Many Jewish people were held captive in Babylon until 538 BCE when the Persians conquered Babylonia and allowed the Jews to return to Palestine. During this period the Jews seem to have incorporated many Mesopotamian beliefs about

Egregorials into their own historical experiences. And so it is now we follow these fascinating ideas as they move westwards and forwards in time.

Biblical Judaism

The Book of Enoch (also known as 1 Enoch) is an ancient Jewish religious work thought to have been written around 300 BCE. Curiously, this was not included in the Hebrew Bible, and by the 4th century CE it had been excluded from the Christian version as well. Interestingly, the book is considered scripture by the Ethiopian Orthodox Church and the Eritrean Orthodox Church.

Central to the Book of Enoch is a description of how a group of entities known as the Watchers came down from the heavens and became involved in the affairs of humanity. In the original Greek translation of the official Bible, the Aramaic word *iyr*, meaning "wakeful one" or "watcher", was translated into the Greek equivalent word, *egregoros*, meaning "wakeful" or "watching". Two hundred of these beings descended to earth on Mount Hermon, now on the border of the modern-day states of Syria and Lebanon. This location had been a sacred place to the Canaanites before the invasion of the Hebrews. Indeed, this tradition continued when shrines to the gods Baal, Zeus, Helios and Pan were built there.

The Book of Enoch describes how the initial group of Watchers that arrived on Mount Hermon quickly noticed how beautiful human women were and soon started breeding with them to create a race of hybrids. These half-angelic, half-human offspring, known as the Nephilim, are also referred to in the official version of the Old Testament:

> The Nephilim were in the earth in those days, and
> also after that, when the sons of God came in unto the
> daughters of men, and they bore children to them; the
> same were the mighty men that were of old, the men of
> renown. (Genesis 6.4)

With regard to our enquiry into non-human intelligences, the important point is that the Watchers taught human beings the creative arts and science, together with the celestial secrets of true heavenly *gnosis*, literally translated from the Greek as "knowledge".

For example, the Watcher known as Azâzêl taught men to forge swords and make shields and breastplates as body armour. He also taught them metallurgy and how to mine from the earth and put different metals to practical uses.

To the women he taught the art of making bracelets, ornaments, rings and necklaces from precious metals and stones. He also showed them how to "beautify their eyelids" with kohl, and he trained them in cosmetic tricks to attract and seduce the opposite sex.

The Watchers also feature in the official version of the Old Testament. It was a Watcher who appeared to Nebuchadnezzar in a dream:

> I was looking in the visions in my mind as I lay on my bed, and behold, an angelic watcher, a holy one, descended from heaven. (Daniel 4.13)

Later, in verse 17, it is explained that the Watchers are angelic beings that keep an eye on humankind and report back to God on what His subjects are up to. As God is supposedly omniscient, this is rather a pointless task:

> This sentence is by the decree of the angelic watchers.
> And the decision is a command of the holy ones,
> > In order that the living may know
> > That the Most High is ruler over the realm of mankind,
> > And bestows it on whom He wishes
> > And sets over it the lowliest of men. (Daniel 4.17)

Going back to the narrative of the Book of Enoch, we find an interesting moral dimension. It seems that although the

Watchers willingly gave humanity many gifts of knowledge, the beneficiaries used it merely to wage warfare and to fall into a state of lawlessness. Such was the chaos that the archangels Michael, Uriel, Raphael and Gabriel felt obliged to inform God about what was going on. God's response was the Great Flood. Ironically, it seems that it was Watcher technology that allowed Noah to build his Ark and save a small number of human beings and many animal species.

For the sin of giving humanity *gnosis*, Azâzêl was bound head and foot and thrown into a deep hole in the desert.

Legend has it that after the Flood the half-human, half-egregorial Nephilim became entities entirely of spirit – incorporeal beings. Humanity had become the main focal point of God's attention. This led the Nephilim to despise humanity and to seek their revenge. The Book of Enoch describes this in some detail:

> But now the giants who are born from the [union of] the spirits and the flesh shall be called evil spirits upon the earth, because their dwelling shall be upon the earth and inside the earth. Evil spirits have come out of their bodies. Because from the day that they were created from the holy ones they became the Watchers; their first origin is the spiritual foundation. They will become evil upon the earth and shall be called evil spirits. The dwelling of the spiritual beings of heaven is heaven; but the dwelling of the spirits of the earth, which are born upon the earth, is in the earth. The spirits of the giants oppress each other, they will corrupt, fall, be excited, and fall upon the earth, and cause sorrow. They eat no food, nor become thirsty, nor find obstacles. And these spirits shall rise up against the children of the people and against the women, because they have proceeded forth [from them]. (1 Enoch 15)

Of course, this account is simply a legend, but in most legends there is a kernel of truth. Here again, as with shamanistic beliefs, we have non-human entities whose origins are the heavens but who now exist within the dark places and who can corrupt and manipulate the minds of humanity.

As well as the Babylonian Captivity, the Bible also describes how the Jewish people were held captive by a later Middle East civilization, the ancient Egyptians. It is to the land of the pharaohs that we now turn our attention.

According to the Bible, the Jewish people had been subjugated in Egypt for many generations. Sadly, there is no archaeological evidence to support the idea that they were ever in Egypt. A prolonged Egyptian stay should have left Egyptian elements in the material culture, such as the pottery found in the early Israelite settlements in Canaan, but there are none. This suggests that the Book of Enoch is purely Hebrew and Sumerian in its influences. But of course, in ancient times, particularly in the Middle East, cultures regularly shared ideas and customs. It is fair to conclude that such cross-fertilization would also have occurred between the Jewish people and those located along the Nile river, and this is where our review now takes us.

Ancient Egypt and Greece

In ancient times all civilizations in the ancient Near East shared not only trade but also ideas and philosophies. For example, in his book *The Rise of the West*, William McNeill gives examples of how Sumerian art influenced art in ancient Egypt. It is also intriguing to discover that Sumerian cylinder seals have been found in Egyptian tombs. Of course, the most obvious link is the clear similarities between Mesopotamian ziggurats and the early Egyptian step pyramids. From this it is reasonable to suggest that if art, architecture and funerary objects were shared between these two cultures, then philosophy and theology would have been similarly cross-fertilized.

One of the most culturally significant battles in the ancient world took place in 1457 BCE in a place called Megiddo. This was a direct conflict between the Egyptians under Thutmose III and the Mesopotamian Syrians. What is intriguing here is that the name Megiddo is from the Hebrew Har-Meggido (Mount of Megiddo), which in turn is translated into Greek as *Armageddon*. As many of my readers will know, according to the biblical Book of Revelation this is where the final battle between the good and evil Egregorials will take place.

The ancient Egyptian creation myth involved a single creator-entity, known as Temu. From his semen were created two children, a brother and a sister, Shu and Tefnet. These two, in turn, created Geb (the earth god) and Nut (the sky goddess). From the union of Geb and Nut came Osiris, Isis, Seth and Nephthys.

Here again we have a similar myth to the Sumerian tale of the Annukai and the Watchers, with sexual union between entities from the sky (in the role of Nut) and from the Earth (in the guise of Geb). From this union comes a race of hybrids who begin to teach humanity the skills needed to bring about civilization. In Egyptian tradition the guides were Osiris and his sister-wife Isis.

But all was not well. The brother of the twin-consorts, Seth, was unhappy with his siblings and murdered Osiris, leaving Isis grief-stricken. Osiris's body was dismembered into 14 pieces and Seth had these distributed across the world. Isis successfully finds all but one of the parts (his penis) and is able to reassemble Osiris, who comes back to life as immortal.

As we have seen, this dismemberment and reconstitution of the body is a central theme of shamanic travelling. And here we find exactly the same theme in the ancient Egyptian creation myth. Can this be simply coincidence? Or is it a reflection of a deeper truth within all cultures, irrespective of location?

The other great shamanic belief, that there are non-human entities that can influence and even possess human beings, has been recorded for as long as there have been written records. An Egyptian inscription found at the Temple at Thebes, dated around 400 BCE, tells of a Syrian princess who had been possessed by an alien intelligence:

> Then came the god of the abode of Bint-Reschid; having communicated his virtue [as an exorcist] to her said in the presence of Chrons, the counsellor of Thebes, "Be thou welcome, great god who drivest out rebels; the town of Bachtan is thine, the peoples are thy slaves, I myself am thy slave. I will return from whence I came."

Note that the entity states that it will return "from whence I came", suggesting there is a particular place that it normally inhabits.

One of the closer cultural relationships was that between ancient Egypt and ancient Greece. It is known from archaeological finds that as far back as the Early Bronze Age (c3000 BCE) the Minoans of Crete were trading with the Egyptians. However, it was only from the 7th century BCE that substantial and close relations developed between mainland Greece and Egypt. As with the cross-fertilization of ideas between Mesopotamia and Egypt, a similar cultural linkage can be made between Egypt and Greece, none more so than in religious ritual and burial customs. It seems that an understanding of the egregorial world continued to move westward.

By the 6th century BCE large numbers of Greeks were living and working in Egypt and a fully Greek city, Naucratis, had been founded on the Nile river, 70 kilometres (45 miles) from the open sea. Three hundred years later the Greek general Alexander the Great conquered Egypt, which effectively became part of the Greek world.

It is fair to conclude that many ancient Greek tales regarding the Underworld and its inhabitants were taken from Egyptian mythology. For example, the Osiris myth discussed earlier has many parallels with the later Greek myth of Persephone and Demeter. Here we have an abduction into the Underworld as well as encounters with entities not of this world but from another, darker place that can overlap into our earthly realm.

Ancient Egyptian magical practices were also adopted by the Greeks. Indeed, it has been observed that the Greeks took Egyptian magic and turned it from a system into a technology. One specific system-cum-technology was a process known as Goetia. The ancient Greek word *goēteía* means "charm, jugglery, sorcery" from *góēs*, meaning "sorcerer, wizard" (plural: *góētes*). The Greeks realized that certain systematized techniques could be used to make direct contact with non-human entities.

It is important to recognize that the religion of the ancient Greek mainland (which is, in effect, the tip of the greater Balkan peninsula) would have been a form of shamanism brought down from the north by various invading groups. These beliefs would have encountered ideas facilitated by the sea trade with the Middle East and North Africa.

The mixture of shamanism and polytheism brought about a creation myth that has significant similarities with that of the Egyptians, the Sumerians and, through the Book of Enoch, the Jews. Yet again we have a group of giants who came to earth from the sky. These were the Titans, the progeny of a union between Gaia (Earth) and Uranus (Sky). Note again the hybridization taking place here, similar to the Egyptian union of Nut (Sky) and Geb (Earth) and the Jewish legend of the "giants who are born from the [union of] the spirits and the flesh" as described in the Book of Enoch.

Moreover, the similarities continue. According to Greek mythology the Titans rebelled against their father Uranus, were expelled from "heaven" (by Zeus) and shut up in the Underworld (Tartarus). We are immediately reminded of the Enûma Eliš, the Babylonian creation myth which describes that after a great revolt in heaven the giant Anunnaki were banished into the Underworld.[4] The Greek word *titanos* actually means "grey", which is something we will return to later.

Earlier we discussed a terrifying Mesopotamian Egregorial known as Inanna. This entity would visit her victims at night, bringing all forms of night terrors. The ancient Greeks had their own variation of this being: a number of nocturnal vampire-like creatures called the *lamiae*. These would prey on young men, steal their semen and drink their blood. Fear of these creatures can still be found in Greek rural communities. Of course, an alternative conclusion can be drawn from such similarities, which is that these encounters describe identical entities manifest in different communities and cultures. Instead of being subject to cross-fertilizing influences, each culture finds its own way to embody universal perceptions.

The next great civilization to rise in the Western world was that of Imperial Rome. This hugely successful empire took as its cultural basis many, if not all, elements of Greek philosophy and theology. It therefore is of great historical significance but adds little to our theme. I should therefore like to pass over the whole Roman and early Christian period of European history and move our enquiry to the days after the fall of the Roman Empire, when Europe and much of the Middle East fell into a period now known as the Dark Ages, followed by the medieval era. As we have discovered, it is in the dark that Egregorials find their natural habitat.

CHAPTER 3
THE MIDDLE AGES

This has proven to be a difficult chapter to write. The reason for this is not lack of subject matter, far from it, but simply the challenge of what centuries to include and what cultures and belief systems to consider. I have taken the easy route by stretching the definition of the "Middle Ages" from the closing years of the Roman Empire to the early days of the Enlightenment. I know this is not technically correct, but it does seem that occult, magical and theological philosophies remained fairly consistent during this extended period of time. It was only when the scientific worldview began taking hold in the late 17th century that humanity started to look at the universe with cold, rational eyes.

I have also taken a largely Western perspective, in part to reflect reliable assumptions about my main readership. However, this in no way means that I do not consider Indian, Chinese and other Far Eastern cultures to have their own Egregorials. In focusing on the Western evidence, I hope I will motivate at least some readers to look further afield eventually and make their own discoveries in the relevant literature.

So let us now move on to the chaos leading up to the Fall of Rome and the so-called Barbarian invasions.

Gnosticism

After the collapse of the Roman Empire, Christianity, although technically the empire's state religion, was far from a singular unit. Many alternative interpretations of the Christian message were abroad, and even the question of what were considered to be "gospel" texts was heavily disputed. For example, as with the Book of Enoch (see pp27–30), some writings were rejected from the official canon because they seemingly contradicted what the Christian authorities believed to be a true reflection of "God's word". One of the major "heretical" groups were the Gnostics.

Although Christian in theological outlook, the Gnostics were heirs to a belief system that had its roots in ancient Greek philosophy. Their thinking in turn became hugely influential on two other groups involved in esoteric thinking: the Jewish Kabbalists and the Islamic Sufis. It is generally recognized that all four philosophies can be termed "Gnostic", in that they all argue that there is a reality behind the one presented to us by our "ordinary" senses. This more superficial reality is a fabricated one that entraps us and denies us access to the greater universe, known as the Pleroma, a term borrowed from 2nd-century BCE Gnostic beliefs. The Greek word *Pleroma* literally means "fullness", from the verb *plero*, "I fill".

Many scholars have argued that the ancient Greek roots of Gnostic thought were grounded in Neoplatonism and possibly even Buddhism. What is fairly clear is that Gnosticism was motivated by a number of philosophers, Jewish, Christian and subsequently Islamic, who could not understand how a supposedly benevolent God could allow the existence of evil. As the central tenet of all Abrahamic religions is that if God is omnipotent, omnibenevolent and omniscient, how can he create evil in any form? This is known as the question of "theodicy". For polytheistic religions such as those of the Sumerians, the ancient Egyptians and the ancient Greeks, such a problem could be explained by the interference in an otherwise perfect world by gods of evil. However, such an escape clause cannot be cited by monotheistic religions such as Christianity, Judaism and Islam. In the 4th century BCE Christian author Lucius Lactantius attributed what has now become known as Epicurus' trilemma to the ancient Greek philosopher Epicurus. In his *De Ire Dei* (The Anger of God), written in the 3rd century CE, Lactantius paraphrases Epicurus:

> God, he says, either wishes to take away evils, and is unable; or He is able, and is unwilling; or He is neither willing nor able, or He is both willing and able. If He is willing and is unable, He is feeble, which is not in accordance with the character of God; if He is able and unwilling, He is envious, which is equally at variance with God; if He is neither willing nor able, He is both envious and feeble, and therefore not God; if He is both willing and able, which alone is suitable to God, from what source then are evils? Or why does He not remove them?[1]

The solution proposed by the Gnostics, under the influence of ancient Greek Platonic and Neopythagorean beliefs and contemporary Jewish thought such as the Merkabah/Merkavah tradition, was a simple one: the God of the Old Testament was a lesser god, one that laboured under the self-deluded belief that he was the True God. This god was known as the Demiurge, from the ancient Greek *dēmiourgos*. This word, meaning "craftsman" or "producer", was first used in a philosophical context in Plato's *Timaeus*, written around 360 BCE. This being created the seemingly physical universe from the blueprint of the Platonic Forms that make up the real universe hiding behind this one. In effect, the Demiurge created an imperfect version of reality and placed humankind and all other known living creatures within this artificial simulation. Later we shall return to the writings of Plato in connection with his famous "cave analogy" (see pp146–7).

The 2nd-century BCE Gnostic philosopher Valentinius argued in his writings that the sensory universe is actually an empty vessel containing nothing but mind-created illusions. This idea had long been suggested in the Indian subcontinent as a central concept of Vedantism. For the Vedic philosophers the illusion is known as Maya. In ancient Greek terminology the opposite of the Pleromic "fullness" is something known as the Kenoma, literally meaning "emptiness".

This emptiness presents itself to an observing consciousness as being full of seemingly material objects – mountains, trees, other people, planets, galaxies. This is what German philosopher Immanuel Kant, in his book *Critique of Pure Reason* (1781), termed the *noumenal* world. But Kant added to this the absolute fact that any observing consciousness can never interact directly with the noumenal world because we actually use our senses to create an inner, brain-created, facsimile of the noumenal. This he called the *phenomenal* world: the world of inner experience.

Judaism

As I have already mentioned, the Merkavah school of early Jewish mysticism was influential on Christian Gnosticism. The word *merkavah* means "something to ride in", and relates to the school's fascination with Ezekiel's vision of a chariot and the true nature of the beings seen by this prophet. Known as the *hayyot*, these were humanoid with four faces: a man, a lion, an ox and an eagle. The *hayyot* also have wings. That this school was extremely influential is evidenced by similar discussions found in many texts of the period, including the famous Dead Sea Scrolls.

The Merkavah universe consists of seven levels. By following certain rituals, a mystic can journey to these various levels, or *hekhal*. This word, incidentally, which means "temple" or "tabernacle", is actually taken from the Sumerian word *akkadian*, or "big house". This suggests that the mystical Jewish concept of higher levels of reality may have been taken from the period of the Babylonian Captivity and incorporated into Merkavah thinking. One of the manuals used to facilitate magical journeys through the *hekhal* is known as the *Maaseh Merkavah*, which also contains instructions for drawing down celestial beings onto the earthly plane. These beings were known as the "Great Angels" and could, if approached correctly, be controlled by the magician.

I cannot help but draw parallels here with the shamanic journey. Both the shaman and the Merkavah traveller journey through various alternative levels of reality and, in doing so, encounter non-human intelligences.

In this period Jewish thought was also influenced by another great religious movement, namely Islam.

Islam

Islam is a major world religion belonging to the Semitic family – that is to say, it shares with the Jewish and Christian religions the Hebrew Bible as a source document. It was promulgated by the Prophet Muhammad in Arabia in the 7th century CE. The Arabic term *Islam* literally means "surrender".

According to Islamic tradition, around 610 CE Muhammad had an encounter with a majestic, non-human entity who was later identified as the angel Gabriel. He then heard a voice announcing that he was the "messenger of God". With regard to the themes of this book, it is the location of this encounter that is significant. It took place in a cave on the northern side of what is now known as Jabal al-Noor (the Mountain of Light), an almost sterile hill of black stone a few miles north of Mecca. The cave, known as Ghar-e-Hira, located almost at the top of the hill, is small and cramped. It was here that Muhammad regularly took himself for periods of seclusion and meditation.

The initial visitation and subsequent announcement perturbed the Prophet, but he was reassured by his wife Khadijah that something of great moment was taking place and that he should open himself to whatever messages he might receive. He then began to receive a series of communications. It has been stated that these messages were not communicated by a voice but appeared directly and voicelessly within his consciousness. Some accounts claim that the only actual sound he heard was a noise like a bell. This is intriguing because, as we shall discover, ringing and bell-like sounds are frequently reported during egregorial encounters. It is important also to note that these communications took place in the darkness of a north-facing cave. Darkness certainly seems to facilitate the opening of the mind to the Pleroma, as we shall see.

What ensued was a series of profound communications which Muhammad wrote down. These revelations, together with later communications he received in the city of Medina, became the Holy Qur'an. A new religion had come into being, one that rapidly spread across the Middle East and north Africa. Its powerful message resonated with many who heard it. It offered a logical and systematic model of the universe. Scientific thought and philosophy were easily assimilated within it. Also, like Christianity with regard to Gnosticism and Judaism with regard to the Merkavah School and the Kabbalists, it developed its own mystical group. These became known as the Sufis. Of specific relevance to many of the ideas described in this book are the writings of the 12th-century Persian Sufi philosopher Sohrawardi and his concept of Nâ-Kojâ-Abâd, the "country of non-where", and the way in which this model of reality was subsequently adapted by the contemporary French Sufi philosopher-linguist Henry Corbin.

Henry Corbin and the Imaginal

In spring 1972 Corbin presented a paper at the Colloquium of Symbolism in Paris. This, in turn, was based on a paper that had appeared eight years before in the Belgian journal the *Cahiers internationaux de symbolisme*.

Corbin introduced to the West a concept he termed *the Mundus Imaginalis*, the world of the image. He had used this term to describe an idea well-known in Iranian Sufi circles which had no equivalent in Latin, French or English. The qualifier, which may be translated as "imaginal", does *not* mean "imaginary" but is far subtler. In French and English "imaginary" equates with things or circumstances that are unreal. For the Iranian philosophers there is a parallel form of reality, a dimension related to, but in no way identical with, the Western concept of a Utopia.

In Persian the idea of Nâ-Kojâ-Abâd, the "country of non-where", goes back to the writings of the Persian sage Sohrawardi in the 12th century. Sohrawardi wrote a series of magical stories in which the central protagonist encounters entities which are not from our everyday reality. These tales are profoundly Gnostic in their underlying philosophy (or, more accurately, theosophy). According to them, this world is an imperfect reflection of another reality that is perfect, the Nâ-Kojâ-Abâd. The entities that originate in Nâ-Kojâ-Abâd are perfect, like Platonic Forms. In the stories these beings are made of pure light, and their home is "beyond Mount Qâf", as we learn from one entity that appears in Sohrawardi's story "The Crimson Archangel".

Sohrawardi pointed out that in our waking lives we exist, for the most part, in what he calls the "terrestrial" – that is, the seemingly consistent physical world that surrounds us. This is the Islamic equivalent of Kant's noumenal world and what the Gnostics called the Kenoma. This is quite literally the "sensible" world. But there is another sensory reality that has both dimension and extension but is not part of the noumenal. This can only be perceived directly by the mind itself under specific conditions. Sohrawardi called this alternative reality the "sidereal". This is the Islamic version of the Gnostic Pleroma. In Arabic the terrestrial, sensible world is known as Molk and the sidereal as Malakut.

These two worlds intersect at what is known in Sufi philosophy as the Alam al-Mithal. This is Corbin's *Mundus Imaginalis*, the world of the image. It is important to stress that Corbin believes this liminal world to be ontologically real. It is perceived via another form of sensory perception, the imaginal.

So, in summation, Corbin's interpretation of Sohrawardi's universe involves a sensible world (the Kenoma of the Gnostics and an equivalent of Kant's noumenal) and an imaginal world (the Gnostic's Pleroma). Both have equal objective reality but are perceived by a different set of senses.

Corbin argues that the *Mundus Imaginalis* can also be apprehended in "the intermediary state between waking and sleeping". The spiritualists of Shi'a Islam call this the "country of the hidden Imam". As we shall see later, modern psychology calls this the hypnagogic state.

Islam's roots are entwined with the fundamental beliefs of Judaism and Christianity, specifically the writings of the Old Testament. With this in mind, it is not surprising that the legend of the Watchers can also be found in Islamic sacred texts. However, the Islamic interpretation has three angels, elected by the larger host of angelic beings, going down to earth to prove to God that angels are superior to human beings. The main two angels were known as Harut and Marut, accompanied by a third angel, our friend Azâzêl, the Old Testament Watcher who taught humanity how to make weapons. But within Islamic tradition Azâzêl was also a member of a curious group of entities inherited from pre-Islamic culture: the djinn.

The djinn

According to the Book of Enoch, the Nephilim became spirits:

> They will become evil upon the earth and shall be called evil spirits. The dwelling of the spiritual beings of heaven is heaven; but the dwelling of the spirits of the earth, which are born upon the earth, is in the earth. (1 Enoch 15)

So here we have a direct link between the Watchers, the Nephilim and the djinn.

The word *djinn* is derived from the Arabic root *jannah*, meaning "hidden". In the Qur'an these entities are referred to as "God's other people". They exist in Corbin's Malakut and break through into the Molk through the "gateway" of the Alam al-Mithal. Using my own terminology, these locations are the Pleroma, the Kenoma and the hypnagogic realm respectively.

According to Arabian traditions there are various types of djinn, described by colour. Of particular interest to our purpose are those Egregorials known as the green djinn and the red djinn. Legend has it that green djinn live in caves and other dark places. Yet again we have the idea that caves and caverns are the liminal locations where such entities can enter this world. Darkness seems to open the portal.

Much more powerful than the green djinn are the greatly feared red djinn. Significant here is that the red variety regularly appear in the guise of snakes or reptiles. They are particularly dangerous and have a deep hatred of humanity. Their sole aim is our destruction.

Various verses in the Qur'an describe how God created humanity out of clay, the angels out of light and the djinn out of the smokeless fire. The three creations have widely different abilities. For example, although created out of light, angels have no free will. They can only do the bidding of God. Humans and the djinn do have free will, which means they can choose to not do God's bidding. Legend has it that God demanded that all the angels and djinn bow down to his human creation, Adam. The leader of the djinn, Azazel (Iblis), refused, arguing that he and his kind had been created out of fire, whereas Adam was simply a creature of clay. For this insubordination Azazel and the djinn that followed him were expelled from Paradise. Here again we have a legend in which a group of Egregorials fall from the sky to earth to become the Watchers.

It is not so surprising that Judaism and Islam have a virtually identical description of how the Watchers came to earth. But the idea that the djinn, as described by Islamic beliefs, are also Watchers prompts some interesting observations about Egregorials in general. For example, we shall discover a great deal of snake and reptile imagery when, later in this book (Chapter 11), we look at drug-facilitated egregorial encounters created by substances such as ayahuasca and dimethyltryptamine (DMT). Similar "reptilian" entities feature in UFO abduction cases on a regular basis. We shall focus on this too in a later chapter. But now, before we move on, there is another curious belief regarding djinn, suggesting that they are responsible for ghosts.

According to modern Islamic scholar Mikayl Yahya ibn Kefa, Muslims believe that every human being has, at birth, a personal djinn allocated to them. This djinn shares your existence with you and witnesses all the events that take place in your life. At death this personal djinn does not die but continues as an independent being. That these djinn also have total memory recall regarding every second of their human partner's life and an ability to shape-shift means that after the death of the human partner they can appear as ghosts of those who have died. They can use their faultless knowledge of the life of their "host" human to give convincing evidence that they are indeed the ghost of that particular person. This is yet another theme that we shall review later, specifically in relation to the theories of American ghost hunter Paul Eno (see p99).

The Watchers, the djinn and the other egregorial entities we have encountered in this chapter all have one thing in common: they originally existed in the heavens, came down to earth, were defeated or banished by a controlling power, and ended up underground to occasionally enter this world through portals such as caves and sink-holes.

What is the significance of otherworldly creatures moving underground? To seek answers to this mystery, as well as related questions, we must now change direction. Thus far we have travelled through time from the late Paleolithic period to the Middle Ages. We now need to switch to a more thematic approach, as the phenomenon seems to split into various specific threads. These are all related, and in what follows there is a great deal of overlapping interpretations.

For our first venture we need to discover more about the Egregorials that became hidden in plain sight, the inhabitants of what is known as the Secret Commonwealth. It is to the furthest edges of the European continent that we take our study.

PART TWO

OVERLAPPING THEMES

CHAPTER 4
THE SECRET COMMONWEALTH

Throughout recorded history the belief that humanity shares this planet with a variety of other sentient entities has been persistent. In the British Isles these beings are known as "fairies".

"Fairy" (or, more accurately, "Faerie") was originally an adjective rather than a noun. It did not refer to a form of elemental creature but was a descriptive term, similar to our present-day "paranormal". The inhabitants of alternative reality in this region were known as the Fay. The word "fairy" also has roots in the Latin *fata*, which means "enchantment". In Middle English the suffix -erie (a place where something is found) was added to the English transliteration of "Fay", Faie, to create the word "Faerie" – the place where fairies dwell.

It is important to note that the imagery of fairies having wings was a creation of Victorian illustrators, with no parallel in real folk traditions. Similarly, the idea that fairies are small is also a product of Victorian romanticism, exacerbated by the Hollywood image devised by Walt Disney and his associates.

Having clarified our terms, we need now to review the evidence that such entities actually exist; or are they simply imaginative fantasies that have no basis in truth?

The Tuatha De Danann
In Irish mythology there exists a group of semi-divine beings known as the Tuatha De Danann ("children of the goddess

Dana"). This is a race of ancient magicians who descended from the heavens to land on the sacred hill of Tara. Here these beings flitted in and out of the two realms on a regular basis, involving themselves directly in the lives of mortals around them. With the coming of Christianity, they were banished into the "hollow hills", becoming known as the "Shining Ones": the Sidhe. Here, yet again, we have a type of magical beings coming down from heaven and, after a period of intermingling with humans, disappearing underground as circumstances changed.

After their defeat, these Irish beings withdrew into the fairy mounds. These mounds were believed to be portals by which mortals can enter the alternative Faerie universes, such as Mag Mell (the Pleasant Plain), Emain Ablach (the Fortress of Apples) and Tír na nÓg (the Land of Youth).

Mag Mell was, for the ancient Irish, a place that was visited after death, or during what we would now call a near-death experience (NDE) or out-of-body experience (OBE). Tír na nÓg is similar – yet another alternative universe. It can be dangerous: Irish legend has it that an enticing creature known as a *leannan sidhe* ("beautiful sweetheart") could lure the unsuspecting mortal here. As in many similar myths from around the world, this other place moves at a totally different temporal speed. On returning from this alien dimension, the abducted person discovers that years have gone by, whereas they seem to have been away only for a few hours or days. In Japanese myth this place is known as Ryūgū-jō, the undersea palace of the dragon god.

Historically, there have been for a long time cultural links between Ireland and the Scottish Highlands and Islands. The term "Scots" actually refers to an Irish tribe. In the early Middle Ages the two were linked in a kingdom known as the Dál Riata. Not surprisingly, we find many similarities between Irish and Scottish folk beliefs regarding the enigmatic beings under scrutiny here.

Robert Kirk

One of the earliest surveys of Scottish fairy folk was that conducted by Scottish clergyman Robert Kirk in the late 17th century. Published in 1691, his book *The Secret Commonwealth* is a fascinating glimpse into a world where the supernatural was simply another aspect of the natural world.

Kirk's first chapter, entitled "Of the Subterranean Inhabitants", focuses particularly on the idea that there was once a race of "earth-dwellers" in the British Isles, and that their artificial caves, known as "fairy hills" or "howes", could easily be found. These entities survive in Scottish folk memory as the legendary "feen".

Andrew Lang, in an introduction to Kirk's *Secret Commonwealth* written in the 19th century, makes the following observation:

> In many ways, as when persons carried off to Fairyland meet relations or friends lately deceased, who warn them, as Persephone and Steenie Steensen were warned, to eat no food in this place, Fairyland is clearly a memory of the pre-Christian Hades.[1]

Even more interesting is Kirk's specific description of the non-human entities:

> These Siths or Fairies they call Sleagh Maith or the Good People [...] are said to be of middle nature between Man and Angel, as were Daemons thought to be of old; of intelligent fluidous Spirits, and light changeable bodies (lyke [sic] those called Astral) somewhat of the nature of a condensed cloud, and best seen in twilight. These bodies be so pliable through the subtlety of Spirits that agitate them, that they can make them appear or disappear at pleasure.[2]

Again we have the familiar theme that these entities are hybrid creatures existing both in the Pleroma and the Kenoma, and that the portals between the two worlds can be found in the darkness of caves and mounds.

Robert Kirk died before he was able to have his book published. Legend has it that he was himself abducted into Fairyland by the Sleagh Maith as a punishment for revealing the secrets of the "Good People". In a journal article entitled "A Prospect of Fairyland", Stewart Sanderson writes that Kirk

> ... was in the habit of taking a turn in his nightgown on summer evenings on the fairy hill beside the manse, in order to get a breath of fresh air before retiring to bed: and one evening in 1692 – 14 May – his body was found lying, apparently dead, on the hill.[3]

Given Kirk's interest in the supernatural, the idea that his soul had been taken into the Underworld, leaving his body to be found next morning, must have been irresistible.

WY Evans-Wentz

In 1911 the American anthropologist Walter Yeeling Evans-Wentz (1878–1965) published a fascinating book entitled *The Fairy-Faith in Celtic Countries*. This was based upon his Oxford University doctoral thesis, which was fed by his extensive anthropological field work in Wales, Scotland, Ireland, Cornwall, Brittany and the Isle of Man. (Many years later Evans-Wentz was to find fame for his translation into English of the *Tibetan Book of the Dead*, published in 1927.)

After reviewing the evidence, Evans-Wentz concludes that records of these Celtic Egregorials (to use my own general term for them) may suggest the existence of a higher reality that can occasionally be glimpsed under certain altered states of consciousness. More importantly, he argues that these beings may have independent existence: in other words, they are not residual race-memories of a reclusive clan of dwarves, or simply hallucinations:

> But in visions by natural seers, following again the theory of our Irish seer-witness, there is present not only an outside force (as seems to be the case when ordinary apparitions are seen) but also a veridical being with a form and life of its own in a world of its own.[4]

There are many intriguing egregorial encounters reported in *The Fairy-Faith in Celtic Countries*, but the ones that really caught my attention were the anecdotes supplied by then living individuals. These events took place in living memory, in an age of science and supposed rationality. As well as those describing the familiar images of fairy folk, there are others that suggest elements of shamanic transformations reminiscent of Graham Hancock's therianthropes (see p13).

Take, for example, this account by someone named Douglas Hyde:

> I myself, when a boy of ten or eleven, was perfectly convinced that on a fine early dewy morning in summer when people were still in bed, I saw a strange horse run round a seven-acre field of ours and change into a woman, who ran even swifter than the horse, and after a couple of courses round the field disappeared into our haggard. I am sure, whatever I may believe to-day, no earthly persuasion would, at the time, have convinced me that I did not see this. Yet I never saw it again, and never heard of anyone else seeing the same.[5]

Other accounts have profoundly shamanistic elements, including this neat cosmological summary by a renowned Irish "seer":

> The shining beings belong to the mid-world; while the opalescent beings belong to the heaven-world. There

are three great worlds which we can see while we are still in the body: the earth-world, mid-world, and heaven-world.[6]

This is startlingly similar to the classic shamanistic model whereby the universe consists of an Upper, Middle and Lower World which overlap in certain places. Surely that such a model is found across so many cultures across both time and distance cannot be simply coincidence?

Evans-Wentz believed that these hidden worlds were arguably real rather than fanciful, posing intriguing implications for our science. He observes:

> Not only do both educated and uneducated Celtic seers so conceive Fairyland, but they go much further, and say that Fairyland actually exists as an invisible world within which the visible world is immersed like an island in an unexplored ocean, and that it is peopled by more species of living beings than this world, because incomparably more vast and varied in its possibilities.[7]

The entities described by Irish witnesses do not always follow the usual pattern. For example, in 1914 in Cork a little girl described encountering a giant fairy-creature with the general shape of a human being. Its skin had the "glistening luminosity of rancid butter that had been left in the sun". Of particular interest here is her description of the eyes as being like "two dark caverns".

Here we have a description of something disturbingly similar to my mother's nocturnal visitor (see p2). You will recall that it was the large black eyes that particularly disturbed her. As we shall discover later, this theme of "huge black eyes" will be encountered time and time again in connection with Egregorials – from UFO abductions to the experiences of those taking psychedelics. This has to be of enormous significance.

The fairy lore revival

Curiously, the carnage of World War I and the subsequent advances in science and technology did not diminish the public's interest in Kirk's Secret Commonwealth. Indeed, an event in 1927 brought about a revival in fairy lore and associated research. This involved the chance meeting of two intriguing and very different personalities: Bernard Sleigh and Quentin A Craufurd.

Bernard Sleigh is best known as a mural painter, stained-glass artist, illustrator and wood engraver, and for writing an intriguing book, *The Gates of Horn* (1926). His art included a cartographical image entitled *An anciente mappe of Fairyland: newly discovered and set forth*, created in 1918 (now in the British Library, London).

Both men, significantly, had experienced heightened states of conscience.

Sleigh's "doors of perception" may have been opened by a brain operation he had in 1897. After this he regularly experienced profound visions and later in life described himself as a psychic.[8]

I have researched the background to this operation. A few years before 1897, Sleigh developed an abscess in his mouth. To deal with this he had his teeth extracted, but this failed to relieve the symptoms. Indeed, within a few days of the extraction he lapsed into delirium and then unconsciousness. A trepanning process was executed by Dr Fred Marsh, senior surgeon at the Birmingham and Midland Ear and Throat Hospital. This treatment was considered to have been given "six hours before it was too late".

On regaining consciousness Sleigh saw two of everything. He was later to comment that he was never sure which of the two images was the "real one". But more intriguing is that soon after recovering he developed powerful hallucinations in which his colour vision suddenly intensified. This affected red and green, but no other colours. The effect could happen at any time. Sleigh was pre-warned about the intensification every time it happened, because it was preceded by a scent he described as "curious and very destructive". What was even stranger, and not really clarified, was an experience he described as vivid "personifications" of people. In all such situations his material surroundings dimmed until his inner vision slowly faded.

These episodes continued throughout Sleigh's life. He believed himself to be "touched", existing in two planes of existence at the same time. His fascination with the magical and the occult, presumably stimulated by these experiences, led him, after World War I, to start a correspondence with Henry Havelock Ellis, the English physician.

In November 1924 Havelock Ellis sent Sleigh a leaflet on the effects of the hallucinogenic drug mescal (peyote). In the attached note he suggested that Sleigh approach Messrs Potter and Clark of Artillery Lane, London, who were selling mescaline by the ounce. This advice he took, then subsequently wrote about his experiences in *The Gates of Horn*. Here we see Sleigh attempting to use peyote to open his "doors of perception" many decades before Aldous Huxley did in 1954.

Quentin Craufurd (1875–1957), on the other hand, was from a very different background to Sleigh. A captain in the Royal Navy, in 1907 he carried out the first ever wireless communication from onboard HMS *Andromeda*. After he retired, he set up a radio laboratory at home. His plan was to communicate with fairies. He believed he had done so after picking up the "sound of harps and bells". Then followed a series of spoken messages in which Craufurd claimed he was given a great deal of information from his fairy friends. These lasted from 1927 to 1932.

These entities described themselves as "marsh fairies". During this period nine beings were in regular contact, and seemed to be able to generate or facilitate poltergeist-like activity around Craufurd's home.

It must be emphasized that Craufurd was far from simply an enthusiastic amateur in electronic communications: he is regularly cited as one of the inventors of the wireless telephone.

The entities explained to Craufurd that, although they were around humans at all times, they remain unheard and unseen, because our minds are not "tuned" into the right frequency to perceive them. As we shall discuss later, this may not be as strange as it sounds: is it consistent with what we know scientifically about radio frequencies, or something similar.

The 1927 meeting between Sleigh and Craufurd took place after Craufurd had been given a copy of *The Gates of Horn* by a friend. He was so intrigued by its contents that he was determined to meet its author and suggest they collaborate on areas of mutual interest. The two men resolved to create a new organization, the Faery Investigation Society. This took a few years to set up, but in 1929, with psychic medium Claire Cantlon as secretary, the London Lodge printed its first newsletter. By this time the society had over 50 members. That year it hosted five lectures, all reasonably well attended.

The society continued to operate until the late 1930s, though with diminishing numbers. It revived again as the Fairy Investigation Society after World War II with a number of famous members, including Walt Disney and Hugh Dowding. In 1950 Marjorie T Johnson became secretary and ran it for around 15 years. In 1955 she decided to run a census of fairy encounters.

It comes as quite a surprise to learn from this census that even in the so-called Atomic Age hundreds of people across the English-speaking world had encountered the Fay.

Nature for many of us today is something outside our everyday lives – an environment for recreation or dog walking, or for passing through in a car, bus or train. Few of us commune directly with nature, in the sense of stopping to truly experience it. However, by opening ourselves more to the natural world, we have a chance of becoming directly aware of the Secret Commonwealth. A productive approach is to spend a night under the stars or rise early and venture alone into wild places. Dawn and twilight are particularly sensitizing times. Shadows are longer, movements are exaggerated, and sound seems to take on a special quality, becoming almost physical in its intensity. Just being still and quiet in nature at such times, closing our eyes and allowing our senses to attune to the ambient atmosphere, can allow us, if we are lucky, to sense an egregorial presence, moving from the Pleroma to the Kenoma. And we are its facilitators.

As part of my research I came across a fascinating article by Canadian parapsychologist Sue Demeter-St Clair in the Canadian journal *PSICAN* (*Paranormal Studies and Inquiry Canada*). Here she cites an experience that an American man had in Williamsville near Buffalo in the northern United States in 1996. I find this section of particular interest:

> I had been walking about ten minutes when, suddenly, I "heard" a kind of sing-song "chanting" in my mind, which "sounded" like a multitude of very sweet, pleasing voices that were all speaking the same words almost simultaneously, in a kind of cascading aural waterfall effect. I had never experienced anything like this before at any time, and the words were, "Don't you see us? We're all around you. We're all around you, don't you see us? Look – don't you see us. [...]" I "heard" the voices for about 90 seconds, and then the voices abruptly stopped.[9]

Earlier in this book, in the Prologue, I discussed my mother's "alien" encounter. A few weeks later I was visiting her. During a perfectly forgettable conversation with me, she suddenly announced that the "children are not singing as much". I was quite puzzled, as this comment was not related in any way to what we were talking about. I paused and asked her what she meant. She explained that for quite a few weeks she had been accompanied by groups of small people who sang to her. These entities she initially described as children, but then corrected herself by saying they were the same height as a child of three or four years of age. What had fascinated her initially was the entities' beautiful "tiny, high-pitched" voices, which harmonized and followed a sequence of loud and soft cadences. This is uncannily reminiscent of the *PSICAN* report quoted above.

At this point I should explain that after my mother's "alien" experience I took her to see the doctor. I suggested that maybe they should investigate a diagnosis of Alzheimer's disease, linked in this instance with a curious and little-known neurological condition known as Charles Bonnet Syndrome. I was aware of this from my own research into altered states of consciousness. The syndrome was first observed by a French physician named Charles Bonnet in 1758 when, in that year, his grandfather, retired magistrate Charles Lullin, began describing a series of totally bizarre hallucinations. Five years earlier, Lullin had had an operation to remove a cataract from his left eye but his eyesight had continued to deteriorate. He then began to report seeing what started as a blue handkerchief with a small yellow circle in each corner. The colourful handkerchief blocked out other objects in his room – an hallucination of exclusion, obliterating part of his visual field. However, he had a degree of control over this experience, for he discovered he was able to make the image disappear by simply moving his eyes to the right.

The cloth was not the only element of the hallucination. The drapes and furniture of his apartment located behind the handkerchief appeared to be covered with a clear brown cloth embroidered with clover leaves. His whole visual reality had been overlaid with something that was not actually there. As if this were not strange enough, moving around the room were several extremely tall young ladies with wonderful, expensively done coiffures. Some, but not all, had on their heads small hat-like containers. It was as if he were glimpsing another world that overlaid his own.

As time progressed, the hallucinations became more elaborate. On one occasion four young girls aged around 12 walked into Lullin's room accompanied by an infant. Unlike the older women encountered earlier, one of these children seemed to acknowledge his presence by smiling at him. The scenes also became more expansive, with outdoor vistas appearing – landscapes with cities in the distance, woodland scenes and, on one occasion, a fountain, its spray dispersed by the wind.

I was convinced that my mother, like Lullin more than 250 years before, was glimpsing another reality that was seeping over into this one. Lullin's youngsters were slightly older than my mother's visitors but, even so, the correspondence was remarkable.

I was correct in my lay diagnosis, as these hallucinations were forerunners of my mother's development of Alzheimer's. The *PSICAN* Williamsville incident presents an almost identical scenario of voices singing, but with a curious twist added on. The next day the witness was on another walk when the following took place:

The voices said, "We're here – come this way, walk this way. We're here," and I looked to my left and saw another path through the woods that led to Ayer Road, which I could plainly see at the end of it. I turned left and walked down the path, still "hearing" the voices, which, as I approached Ayer Road, came to a stop. Ayer is a fairly quiet street but does get some car traffic, and, somewhat stunned and dazed by this new experience, which seemed to validate my experience of the day before, I walked north past the homes using the lip of the road, as there were no sidewalks. Ayer Road curves slightly at various points, and rounding one of these curves, my eyes fell upon a grouping of four garden gnome statues on the front lawn of one of the homes. The statues were traditionally sculpted and done in what I would call a tasteful and "realistic" manner: they weren't the kind of mass-produced cartoonish garden gnomes so prevalent today.[10]

It may be significant that the witness, when asked about any other unusual experiences, cited just one, which took place two years before the gnome experience, in July 1994. In the early morning, in Williamsburg, Brooklyn, he saw an object he described as a green elongated teardrop, or a "minnow" swoop, close to the skyscrapers of Manhattan.

It did not look like "a craft from another planet" or any kind of craft at all. It looked like a clear blown-glass teardrop, as I said, with bright green smoke or liquid swirling inside it, almost the color of antifreeze. There were no other lights on it, no "doors" or panels or windows. Nothing at all to make it look like a "craft". I know this sounds eccentric, but it almost looked like a bright green "cartoon", or "animated", image, superimposed over "reality", like the cartoon characters in *Who Framed Roger Rabbit?*[11]

Recently I received a long message from one of my readers, archaeologist Phil Breach. Phil explained to me just how thin the *horos* (borderland) between the Pleroma and the Kenoma can be.

In 1999 he was working on an enormous archaeological excavation at the future site of Terminal 5 of Heathrow Airport, just to the west of London. The dig was so huge that around 70 researchers and assistants were involved. Because of time constraints, they had all been given accommodation in the magnificent Gothic pile that is Royal Holloway College, in nearby Egham, Surrey. In what spare time they had, Phil and his associates would wander around the surrounding parkland. One particular location became known to them as the "bunny field" because of the huge number of rabbits grazing there.

Phil was staying at the college seven days a week. One Friday evening he decided to experience the bunny field by staying up as late as he could, outside, surrounded by nature. As it was mid-July, the weather was warm, the night fairly short. He went back to his room at 3am for a short nap and was back outside again at 4am, planning to witness the sunrise. By 7am the sun was fully up and the day rapidly warming up. Phil was lost in the overall beauty of his surroundings. Then, quite suddenly:

> … a big shadow coming in from the right zooms over me *very* fast! I whipped about looking for a source. There were no birds in the sky, no trees close enough to harbour any that might've been. I turned back round to settle down again and looked to my right and saw about 50 yards away zooming down the field a grey shadow about 6 feet long, like an amorphous cloud, flying low over the field, and *really* fast. As I turned my head to face the front, another zipped past across in front of me, about the same distance away.

Initially he thought the shadows were being thrown by birds. However, on noticing that they were grey rather than black, he realized something extremely strange was taking place. He concluded that what he was actually seeing were sylphs, mythological spirits of the air. They have long been considered an aerial variation of the Sidhe, a type of egregorial we have encountered already.

But this was far from the end of the story. About a year later Phil was staying in Winchester, a beautiful medieval city in the south of England. In conversation with a fellow Pagan he had recently befriended, he found himself describing his sylph encounter from the year before.

> Now, I specifically remember not telling him where I was when it happened, coz I didn't want to get bogged down with unnecessary detail. All I began with was "I was in a field …" I could've been anywhere in the world. When I'd finished he said, "You weren't anywhere near Runnymede [where the Magna Carta was signed], were you?" I'd been about a mile as the crow flies from Runnymede. My mouth fell open. "Were you at Royal Holloway College?" he asked! Then he pulled aside his jacket: he had a Royal Holloway polo shirt on. He told me that nature spirit experiences were common in that area, and he told me of the faun that lived in the arboretum, and he told me of how the sylphs gather around the Air Forces Memorial at Runnymede.

Then, a few months later, and again quite by chance, a friend of Phil's gave him a copy of a book entitled *Faeries at Work and Play*, written by 1920s clairvoyant Geoffrey Hodson. Reading Hodson's perceptions of sylph-like entities in the north of England, he was taken aback by the description of a particular sylph encounter near Thirlmere, in the Lake District:

> I cannot make out any distinct shape; they take and lose many different forms, with great rapidity: there is a general suggestion of wing-like formation and occasionally the likeness of a human face or head. Again this appearance is lost, and they appear like wisps of white cloud. The swiftness of movement, and the rapidity with which they change their appearance, make it difficult to study them with any degree of accuracy […] Their movement is not unlike that of swallows flying over the surface of a river […] their colouring is chiefly white, deepening to dove-grey.

In his extensive message to me, Phil finished off with this powerful observation:

> To sum it all up, I think I saw lake spirits that day, still perhaps tied to their element of a lake that had physically gone, but etherically remained: dove-grey (that was the exact colour!) spirits, or the shadows of spirits or something I don't quite know what. I didn't see faces, only amorphous, cloudlike wisps, but I saw them that day, and lastly, and most significantly for me, they saw me first and flew over me and drew my attention to them. They wanted me to see them!

Here we have an extraordinary experience taking place in the most ordinary of circumstances and locations: a field near Heathrow Airport. Indeed, what particularly intrigues me about this incident is that the location of Phil's encounter was later to be enclosed by the vast building that is Heathrow Airport's Terminal Five. Are the sylphs still there flitting invisibly through the air above the serried ranks of check-in desks? This is, indeed, an attractive thought.

Phil Breach's reference to the writings of Geoffrey Hodson stimulated me to check out this author's work. I was delighted to discover that this World War I tank commander, recommended for the Military Cross for his bravery under fire, experienced in his life a series of encounters closely reflecting the themes of our enquiry.

Hodson experienced what is known as a Kundalini awakening when a young boy. He describes this in his *Occult Dairy*:

> I was perhaps only five or six years old [...] It seemed that from within the sun itself, a huge birdlike figure of fire, with a long tail shaped like that of a lyre bird, descended and entered my whole body through the crown of my head, almost setting up a blazing fire within me.[12]

The word *Kundalini* is of Sanskrit origin and literally means "coiled one". In Hinduism (specifically the school of Hinduism known as Shaktism) it is believed that there is a form of divine energy located at the base of the spine, which can be released spontaneously or through extensive practice of yoga or meditation. It seems that in the young Hodson this happened spontaneously. Once released, this energy opens up the senses, allowing the experiencer to perceive a far broader area of reality – or in the terms of our discussion, to perceive those parts of the Pleroma that overlap into the Kenoma.

Hodson believed that what had descended into his young body was a *deva*, another Sanskrit term, meaning "shining being", a form of angel. Over a period of years he was being prepared for communication from an entity calling itself Bethelda, an archangel-like *deva* that was to become Hodson's lifelong teacher.

Hodson was not the instigator of these communications. The entities decided to contact *him*. But throughout history there have been individuals who have actively sought communication with non-human intelligences through ritual and other processes. These individuals are generally grouped together under the term "magicians". By using spells and other occult paraphernalia, magicians have hoped to not only communicate with the egregorial realm, but also manipulate this experience for their own advantage. It is to this topic that we now turn our attention.

CHAPTER 5
THE OCCULT

The word "occult" has its roots in the Latin word *occultus*, which means "hidden" or "secret". In effect, this refers to information about the true nature of the universe that is hidden from the masses or those outside a particular esoteric group. Involved in occultism were individuals or societies wishing to control nature and, more specifically, non-human entities which, it was believed, had exactly the powers sought by the occultists themselves.

Such beliefs and practices have occurred in all human societies throughout recorded history. The Western strand of occultism grew out of the Hellenistic traditions, originating in the Greek-speaking world which stretched from the Middle East to Sicily and various port cities on the coast of north Africa. Complementing and in many cases merging with the Greek tradition was Jewish mysticism, which had similarly spread across the Mediterranean and into Spain.

It was this fertile mixture of ideas and supposedly ancient writings that fascinated many philosophers and intellectuals in Western Europe during the medieval period. This where our enquiry now takes us.

Medieval magic

Our discussion of the Middle Ages (Chapter 3) touched upon the huge influence Jewish mysticism had on European occultism. Particularly significant in relation to the impact of these ideas on 20th-century mysticism is a supposedly ancient book of spells and incantations (technically known as a "grimoire"): *The Book of Abramelin*. This tells the story of an Egyptian magician called Abraham, or Abra-Melinm, who taught his secrets to Abraham of Worms, a Jewish mystic who lived from around 1360 to 1458.

The first printed manuscripts of this work can be dated to around 1608, with two copies now located in Wolfenbüttel in northern Germany.

The main fascination of this book is its central focus on a step-by-step process whereby the magician, after months of purification, fasting and intense prayer, can attain union with an entity described as the "Holy Guardian Angel". *The Book of Abramelin* is not explicit about the true nature of this being, but does make it clear that the entity is uniquely linked to each individual: the magician cannot be spiritually complete until union with his or her Holy Guardian Angel has taken place; and similarly the Holy Guardian Angel cannot be a complete angelic unit without being in union with its human counterpart. (As an aside, anyone who has read my book *The Daemon: A Guide To Your Extraordinary Secret Self*, is likely to find this of particular interest.)

As we shall see later, *The Book of Abramelin* has proven hugely popular with many 20th-century mystics and occultists, including the infamous Aleister Crowley.

In the period between the death of Abraham of Worms in 1458 and the first publication of *The Book of Abramelin* in 1608, the most influential occultist was, without doubt, Heinrich Cornelius Agrippa von Nettesheim. Because one of his key ideas foreshadows *The Book of Abramelin*, it is worth backtracking a little to consider Agrippa here.

Agrippa was born on 14 September 1496, in Cologne, Germany. He is best known for his 1533 publication, *De Occulta Philisophia Libri Tres* (Three Books of Occult Philosophy). The first book is on natural magic; the second on celestial magic; and the third on ceremonial magic.

In Agrippa's universe there were three levels of reality. These were the elementary, the celestial and the intellectual. The elementary world is the physical world that surrounds us here on earth. The celestial is the realm of the planets and stars. The intellectual is the abode of the angels and spirits. Agrippa believed that magic allowed a practitioner in the elementary world to control an entity existing in a higher world. In doing so they could reverse the normal hierarchy of control, using the power of the spirit being to shape events here on earth.

Central to Agrippa's philosophy of magic was the idea that it was the magician who used higher spiritual beings for their own purposes, not the spiritual beings who controlled the magician. The process was to ensure that these entities do one's bidding. This is exactly what is stated in *The Book of Abramelin*. It is probably this approach that attracted one of the most intriguing characters of Tudor England, the enigmatic Dr John Dee.

John Dee and Enochian magic

As we have already seen, the non-biblical Book of Enoch contains a large amount of information on the beings I have termed Egregorials. This was not lost on the magicians and mystics of the Renaissance and Enlightenment, particularly John Dee.

John Dee was born on 13 July 1527 in London. After attending school in Chelmsford, Essex, he entered St John's College, Cambridge, where he graduated in 1546. His academic reputation was such that he was offered a fellowship at the newly founded Trinity College. He had also gained a reputation for being a man of great technical ability. It was recorded that in 1546, for a production of Aristophanes' play *Peace* he created a startling stage effect: the illusion of a huge flying dung beetle carrying off one of the actors. This prompted a good deal of discussion as to whether Dee had applied occult knowledge to achieve this. He added to this mystery by describing the process behind this effect as "thaumaturgy", the capability of a magician to work miracles. This reputation led to Dee's arrest by the officials of Queen Mary on the charge of "casting horoscopes". This was soon upgraded to treason. However, he managed to exonerate himself.

In the early years of the reign of Elizabeth I, Dee disappeared from the historical records for five years. Legend has it that he used this time to travel around Europe acquiring knowledge of the Kabbala. This may be evidenced by the fact that in 1564 he published a mystical book with Kabbalistic themes, entitled *Monas Hieroglyphica* (The Hieroglyphic Monad). In this work he presented a curiously modern interpretation of reality, suggesting that at its base level everything is a unity ("monad"). He used as the basis of his discussion a mysterious symbol to show this unity in a graphical shorthand. After his return to England, he moved out of central London to take residence in his mother's old house in Mortlake, a small village to the west of the city.

A decade before, in 1553, a French scholar Guillaume Postel published a book called *De Originibus*. In it he relates meeting an Ethiopian priest. The priest told Postel about the Book of Enoch, which had been lost to Europeans for centuries but had been known by the Ethiopians. It contained Enoch's own record of the language of God, known as the Adamite language. This was the language that came from the mouth of God and had not been corrupted by the Fall. Whoever rediscovered this language would rediscover the key to divine knowledge. Dee owned a copy of *De Originibus*, which has survived the predations of time. It is significant that the sections concerning the Ethiopian priest's testimony have Dee's own handwritten notes scrawled all over them. These notes suggest that Dee was keen to find a way of using this language to control spirits and demons. But first he had to open up communication with them.

Of the many tools used by magicians to communicate with non-human intelligences, one of the most popular is a process known as "scrying". This involves a person looking into any transparent or reflective surface in which scenes and images may be perceived. Particularly popular were black mirrors made of highly polished obsidian, a volcanic glass. This process may have been used in biblical times. In a number of verses in the Old Testament the Children of Israel use devices termed the "Urim and "Thummim" to gain in-depth information and discover the will of God.

Dee himself had tried this technique but was disappointed to find that it did not work effectively for him. In his diary he describes how, in May 1581, he glimpsed what he thought was an angel in one of his crystals; then, in November of the following year, he saw an entity that described itself as the angel Uriel. However, it was only when he teamed up with the mysterious Edward Kelley in 1582 that communications between Dee and a number of Egregorials really began.

It seems that Kelley was an extremely effective scryer. Why this was so is unclear, but it does seem that he had genuine mediumistic skills. The Dee–Kelley collaboration seems to have been a very effective one. Dee was conversant with the processes and procedures of magic and owned a number of scrying facilitators known as "speculums". These were mirrors of highly polished obsidian. He also owned two extremely expensive crystal balls. It is reasonable to conclude that such tools were way beyond the financial reach of the mysterious Edward Kelley.

Right up to 1582 Dee had employed a number of scryers but none had been effective enough for his purposes. On Thursday 8 March 1582 a Mr Clerkson turned up at Dee's house accompanied by a young man he introduced as "Edward Talbot". This was actually Edward Kelley, who for some still unknown reason wished to be known under a different name. Clerkson was effectively a supplier of scrying talent. On introducing Kelley to Dee, he explained how exceptionally effective Kelley's skills were. The two visitors left, but next morning Kelley was back, this time on his own. He announced that he was very keen to work with Dee, whose work he deemed to be serious and worthy of support. Dee brought out one of his crystal balls and requested that the young man work with it to see what he could perceive within its surface. Dee retired to his small private chapel adjoining his study, leaving Kelley alone in the study to do what he could. Fifteen minutes later Dee heard cries from the next room: Kelley had seen something.

Returning to the study, Dee saw Kelley staring into the crystal ball. Looking up, he announced that within the glass he had seen a figure he believed to be the Archangel Uriel.

Uriel was a Watcher, as mentioned in the Book of Enoch. In this role he was the angel who warned Noah about the impending flood. Not only this but, more importantly for our purposes, Enoch also describes how Uriel was involved in the fate of Azazel, leader of the djinn in Islamic tradition, and of Semjâzâ, leader of the Nephilim.

Dee was keen to ask Uriel direct questions about the meaning of another document in his possession, a copy of the *Book of Soyga*. His journal entry is the first time he mentions this book, but it was clearly of great importance to him, because the first question Dee asked Uriel through the mediumship of Kelley was "Is my *Book of Soyga* of any excellency?" Then came the reply: "That book was revealed to Adam in paradise by the good Angels of God."

This proved to Dee something he had long suspected, that his precious copy of the *Book of Soyga*, with its mysterious language, number tables and 36 tablets of letters, was of great mystical importance.

Dee asked if Uriel could give him instructions on how to read the tables of Soyga. Uriel said he could indeed do this but that "only Michael can interpret that book".

Later that same day, Uriel informed Dee that his house was haunted by a spirit calling itself Lundrumguffa. This elemental had been causing trouble there for some time, including injuring Dee in the shoulder the year before. It is important to realize that this information was being conveyed by Kelley to Dee. The question has to be asked, if Kelley was simply making things up, how did he know that Dee had suffered a painful shoulder a year previously: remember, he had only arrived at Dee's house the day before.

They agreed to close the session and start again the next day. At 3pm, as Kelley stared into the stone, he reported seeing a magnificent being wearing a long purple robe spangled with gold. They both assumed this was Uriel. But the being was then attacked by another creature and exposed as a hairy monster, Lundrumguffa himself. The attacker was Uriel. "Michael" then appears.

There is then a series of communications from Uriel and Michael. On Sunday 29 April 1582 Kelley is shown by Michael an elaborate table of numbers. Kelley then spends three hours reading out the contents of the tables, cell by cell, letter by letter. Then there is the incident of "Michael" telling Kelley to go against his profession and marry. This suggests that Kelley was a Catholic priest, which may help explain Kelley's subterfuge in introducing himself to Dee and others under the false name of Edward Talbot.

There was a fall-out between Dee and Kelley, prompted by Dee's wife. Then, on 13 July 1582, the scryer disappeared, only to return again in November announcing he was Edward Kelley and not Edward Talbot. Dee seemed to simply accept this. Perhaps he made allowances because Kelley was an exceptional medium and such skills were hard to come by.

On 21 November 1582 a new spirit called "King Camera" appeared, holding a rod of black and red to "measure us and our power". All this is described to Dee by Kelley. However, King Camera then manifests an object "as big as an egg" held in the hands of a child-sized angel. Dee goes over to where the object is supposed to be. Although he could not see the object or angel, he does see a shadow on the ground, "roundish and less than the palm of my hand. I put my hand down upon it and felt a thing cold and hard."[1] This is a new magical lens that will help Kelley have even greater visions.

On 24 March 1583 the archangel Raphael appears in, I assume, the new magical lens. On the 26th, in the role of *Medicina Dei* (Medicine of God), the entity calling itself Raphael produces the golden book again and points to a series of characters, 21 in total. Dee writes these down. They are the letters of the Celestial Alphabet, the written language of God.

Raphael then makes a curious statement:

> The corners and straights of the earth shall be measured to the depth; and strange shall be the wonders that are creeping in to new worlds. Time shall be altered, with the difference of day and night. All things have grown to their fullness.[2]

Dee claims to have been stunned by this revelation. He had been secretly working on a highly sensitive government report responding to the fact that Pope Gregory XIII had decreed that ten days would be removed from October 1582 to realign the Julian calendar. It was impossible for Kelley or the Egregorial to know this. As this incident is recorded in Dee's private diary, it is highly unlikely that he is being anything but truthful. Indeed, there was a second seemingly telepathic reference concerning one of Dee's associates, Adrian Gilbert, who had been secretly involved in a planned journey to the "new world" of America. Again, how could the entity know this, except by genuine clairvoyance?

In early April 1583 a theme that regularly occurs in egregorial encounters – namely, elements of the ridiculous – starts to muddy the waters. A new entity opens up communication. Kelley describes him as being dressed like a fool from a play. It is important to note that although Dee is keen to open up communication with this being, Kelley is not. In the original transcript of his *Book of Mystery*, Dee writes:

> … but I did carefully ponder the pith of the words which he spake: and so forbare to write very much which he

spake at the beginning by reason EK did so much mislike him, and in a manner toke him to be an illuder.[3]

"Illuder" means deceiver, someone who cannot be trusted. I cannot but observe that if Kelley were deceiving Dee in these communications, why would he offer such reservations about something he himself was creating?

In response to Dee's questioning as to who the creature is, Kelley describes the being opening his chest and showing, inscribed on his exposed heart, the word "El". Dee assumes this is the entity's name and engages in conversation.

Dee was still keen to know the whereabouts of his now lost *Book of Soyga*. In response to a question about this, El speaks the words "Soyga alca miketh".[4] Dee asks what language El is speaking. The answer, to Dee anyway, is of great significance. El replies that it is "a language towght in paradise", confirming that this was the tongue spoken by God to Adam. Dee quickly concludes that this would have been the original language of the Book of Enoch. Not only this, but El promises that within 28 days the Book of Enoch in its original language would be in Dee's possession.

On 4 May there was another peculiar incident, which again suggests that Kelley was a genuine medium. In his diaries Dee describes how Kelley had experienced a series of disturbing visions. One of these occurred as the two men were having supper. Kelley suddenly stops eating and announces that he can see an ocean full of many ships and then a single image of a woman having her head cut off.

Next day, in a scrying session facilitated by Kelley, Dee asks Uriel what Kelley's dream signified. The response is immediate. Referring to the ships, Uriel states:

The one did signify the provision of foreign powers against the welfare of this land, which they shall shortly put into practice. [...] The other, the death of Mary Queen of Scots. It is not long unto it.[5]

Now, if this occurred as described by Dee, then only two alternative conclusions can be made: either Uriel, or whatever Egregorial was pretending to be Uriel, was precognitive; otherwise, if Kelley was pretending to be in communication with spirits, then he himself was precognitive. Of course, there is a third option, which is that Dee made the whole incident up, or exaggerated it. But this seems improbable when a person writes a diary for personal reference, not for publication or to be read by others.

John Dee died in 1608, largely forgotten. Just before his death he took some of his notebooks and locked them in a chest. Others he buried in various locations in the fields around Mortlake. A couple of decades later these buried documents were found by Sir Robert Cotton. Then, in 1622, a gentleman named Robert Jones noticed an odd rattle in an old chest he had bought. On inspection he found a secret drawer. On prising it open, he found a number of Dee's books, papers and a necklace. In a really sad turn of events, a household servant, finding the papers, used a number of them to line her cake tins. In 1672 the remainder of the papers were sold to Elias Ashmole, a wealthy collector. Some of papers were subsequently published as Dee's *Liber Mysteriorum* (Book of Mysteries). The others can now be found in the documents collection of the British Museum, among what is known as the Harleian Manuscripts.

For anyone with an interest in esoteric magic, the most important outcome of Dee's work was his rediscovery of the Enochian Calls, a process, it is believed, by which non-human entities can be evoked and, more importantly, controlled.

An important outcome of Dee's encounters with non-human intelligences was his decipherment of what was to become known as Angelical, the Enochian language. Dee believed this was the language used by God to create the world – and the medium of communication used by the Watchers, the enigmatic entities discussed earlier (see p27). After the disclosure of the 21 characters by *Medicina Dei* on

26 March 1583, Kelley began receiving a series of texts in Angelical. This resulted in a book containing 49 letter tables, each consisting of 49 by 49 letters. The book was known as the *Liber Loagaeth* (the Book of the Speech of God).

A year later the basis of Enochian vocabulary was received by Kelley. This time, uniquely, the entities also gave an English translation. This consisted of 48 *Claves Angelicae* (Angelic Keys), also known as the "48 Calls".

It was these manuscripts, and specifically the Enochian Calls, that fascinated a number of late 19th-century and early 20th-century individuals who wished to gain occult knowledge and power for themselves. One of these ambitious souls was the infamous Great Beast, Aleister Crowley.

Aleister Crowley

If you asked a member of the public to name one famous occult practitioner, I am sure that the vast majority in the English-speaking world would come up with Aleister Crowley. Even now, more than seven decades after his death in an obscure Hastings boarding house, the name immediately evokes images of wild black magic ceremonies and the numbers 666.

Crowley was born in Leamington Spa, a town in the English Midlands, in 1875. His family were members of a particularly strict Protestant sect, the Plymouth Brethren. Always the rebel, Crowley soon broke ties with his parents' fundamentalist beliefs and began his own journey into esoteric spirituality. Such was his mother's dislike of his move away from Christianity that she called him the "Beast of the Apocalypse".

After leaving Cambridge University without a degree, he tried his hand at being a poet before, in 1898, joining an occult brotherhood known as the Hermetic Order of the Golden Dawn. This had been founded ten years earlier by three Freemasons – William Woodman, William Wynn Wescott and Samuel Liddell "MacGregor" Mathers. This was the same

MacGregor Mathers who would, three years later, translate from the original German *The Book of the Sacred Magic of Abramelin the Mage*.

It was this book that really caught the attention of the young occultist. In 1899, with money inherited from the death of his father, Crowley had purchased a large house on the shores of Loch Ness in Scotland. He felt that this place, Boleskine House, would be the ideal location for him to explore some of the ceremonies detailed in *Abramelin the Mage*. With the assistance of his friend and fellow member of the Golden Dawn, Allan Bennett, Crowley began the six-month-long ritual needed to facilitate the appearance of his "Guardian Angel". Having started the procedure, he had to curtail it when he was called back to London by Mathers on some urgent Golden Dawn business. He later returned to the ritual in 1906 on an extended honeymoon with his new wife, Rose, and completed the arduous practice, by his own account, while the couple were travelling together.

It is recorded that Crowley took the power of *The Book of Abramelin* extremely seriously, specifically the fourth book which describes how to create a series of magic squares containing letters arranged upon a grid of smaller squares. In an introduction to a recent translation of *The Book of Abramelin*, American occultist Lon Milo DuQuette tells of how Crowley carefully hand-copied a complete set of the squares and had them bound together in an expensive, privately printed folio edition. He often warned his students not to touch this collection without previous preparation.[6]

After spending time in Egypt and then Ceylon, the Crowleys discovered that Rose was pregnant. They decided to return to Egypt rather than travel back to Scotland. While in Cairo, Crowley was keen to show Rose how he could evoke Egregorials, so he performed a ritual known as the "Preliminary Invocation of the Goetia". Readers will recall from our discussion of ancient Greek egregorial rituals (p33) that *goēteía* was a technique used to bring non-human intelligences through from the Pleroma. Much to Crowley's surprise, Rose failed to see any sylphs, but instead fell into a trance and began to vocalize elements of Egyptian ritual magic, then announcing that the god Horus wished to speak with her husband.

Crowley subsequently discovered that it was not in fact Horus at all who wished to open up communication. The entity keen to break through into the Kenoma announced itself as Aiwass. This being informed Crowley that through him a book would be dictated, and this book was to be the basis of a new philosophy.

So what exactly was Aiwass? There is a great deal of conjecture in this regard. According to Crowley's former student Israel Regardie, this entity was simply an aspect of Crowley's own subconscious. Another occultist, Kenneth Grant, argued that Aiwass was an extra-terrestrial from the Sirius solar system.

There may be a much simpler explanation. Crowley described Aiwass as his "Holy Guardian Angel".

It is important at this juncture to reflect on exactly what esoteric thinkers believe to be the role of the "Holy Guardian Angel". In the introduction to his translation of *The Book of Abramelin* McGregor Mathers explains the purpose of this famous book of spells and incantations:

That man is the middle nature, and natural controller of the middle nature between the Angels and the Demons, and that therefore to each man is attached naturally both a Guardian Angel and a Malevolent Demon, and also certain Spirits that may become Familiars, so that with him it rests to give the victory unto the which he will. That, therefore, in order to control and make service of the Lower and Evil, the knowledge of the Higher and Good is requisite [that is, in the language of the Theosophy of the present day, the knowledge of the Higher Self]. From this it results that the magnum opus propounded in this work is: by purity and self-denial to obtain the knowledge of and conversation with one's Guardian Angel, so that thereby and thereafter we may obtain the right of using the Evil Spirits for our servants in all material matters.[7]

In other words, by evoking the assistance of one's own "higher self" one can control Egregorials breaking through into everyday reality from the higher realms (the Pleroma and Kenoma).

In spring 1904 Crowley, after a series of invocations, began to hear a voice which started dictating a series of statements and instructions. After three hours he had written down the first three chapters of what was subsequently to be known as *The Book of the Law* (*Liber AL vel Legis*). It was here that Crowley introduced his concept of "magick": he changed the spelling because he was keen to differentiate occult practices from stage or performance "magic".

It is essential to appreciate that for Crowley Magick "is the science and Art of causing change to occur in conformity with will". By this he meant that the contents of what we have termed the Kenoma can be influenced by the will of a person sufficiently trained. In Greek the word for will is *thelema*, and it was this term by which Crowley's religious and philosophical movement became known.

The concept of "will" has been a central part of philosophical ideas, especially German idealism, for more than two centuries. The classic believer in the "will" was Nietzsche. Magicians believe that human will and divine will are in harmony.

In 1907, with the assistance of George Cecil Jones, another member of the Golden Dawn, Crowley set up his own mystery school which he called the *Argenteum Astrum* (Silver Star). Central to this was Crowley's interpretation of John Dee's Enochian magic, as discussed earlier (p68). In 1909, accompanied by his student Victor Neuberg, Crowley visited Algeria and here, using "Enochian language", he claimed to have evoked the demon Choronzon.

Known as the "dweller in the abyss", this Egregorial has the role of destroying the ego of the magician that has evoked him. In this way Choronzon facilitates enlightenment.

As we have seen, the Enochian Calls, codified by Dee in the late 16th century, were considered to be a powerfully effective means of evoking Egregorials. For me, what is significant is that Crowley's drawings of the entities he encountered, specifically the being known as Lam, look uncannily like the beings depicted in the African and Indian cave paintings discussed at the start of this book (p12) and, of possibly greater significance, the beings encountered during psychedelic "trips" and, of course, my mother's nocturnal visitor.

In early 1918 Crowley was living in an apartment on Central Park West in New York City. He had decided this was the perfect location to try out a series of magical ceremonies known as the Amalantrah Workings. These had, as their central purpose, the evocation of non-human intelligences using the ministrations of a helpful Egregorial known as Amalantrah. In a curiously similar set of circumstances to the relationship between John Dee and Edward Kelley during their encounters with Uriel (see p70), Crowley used the mediumistic powers of his partner Roddie Minor to communicate with any willing Egregorials.

The process involved creating a portal between this world and the next – in our terminology, between the Kenoma and the Pleroma. What came through was a being calling itself "Lam". Referring to his subsequent portrait of this entity, supposedly drawn from life and exhibited in his *Dead Souls* exhibition in Greenwich Village in 1919, Crowley wrote:

LAM is the Tibetan word for Way or Path, and LAMA is He who Goeth, the specific title of the Gods of Egypt, the Treader of the Path, in Buddhistic phraseology. Its numerical value is 71, the number of this book.[8]

Later that year the drawing appeared as the frontispiece to
Crowley's book *Commentary to Blavatsky's The Voice of Silence*.

In his book *Magick in Theory and Practice* Crowley offered
the following piece of advice:

> In this book it is spoken of the Sephiroth and the Paths;
> of Spirits and Conjurations; of Gods, Spheres, Planes,
> and many other things which may or may not exist. It is
> immaterial whether these exist or not. By doing certain
> things certain results will follow; students are most
> earnestly warned against attributing objective reality or
> philosophic validity to any of them.[9]

Here he clearly suggests that entities encountered during
such ceremonies may or may not have objective reality but
are created by an act of will (Thelema). We must be careful in
interpreting these words. What he actually means by "objective
reality" is an existence outside subjective perceptions. This does
not mean that the entities are not real, it's just that they are
not *objectively* real – that is, they do not have a reality outside
the mind of the perceiver. In this respect they fulfil exactly the
demands of my definition of an Egregorial. That is, they are
"mind-created". In my view (in contrast to Crowley's), this
does not deny them an objective reality. This argument can be
taken further by looking at the experiences of Belgian explorer
Alexandra David-Néel.

Alexandra David-Néel and the tulpas

In Tibet these mind-created entities have long been known
as "tulpas". They play a central part in the unique form of
Buddhism practised in this isolated Himalayan location. One
cannot help wondering if this aspect of Tibetan Buddhism is
derived from an older tradition within this ancient kingdom,
known as Bön. This was originally a shamanic folk religion
that over many years became incorporated into the central

beliefs of Buddhism. It gives Tibetan Buddhism an interesting shamanistic colouring, specifically with regards to animism, the idea that life can be found in seemingly inanimate objects, or even created by the act of thought and concentration.

The concept of the tulpa was brought to the Western world by Alexandra David-Néel, an amazing French-Belgian woman who travelled extensively in India, Nepal, Bhutan, China and Japan between 1910 and 1924. In a fascinating life, she converted to Buddhism at the age of 21. In 1895 she was lead singer (*première cantatrice*) at the Hanoi Opera House in French Indochina. In 1904 she married a French-born engineer, Philip Néel, who in 1910 agreed to her taking a "long voyage" of personal discovery. This odyssey lasted 14 years, including a period in the then forbidden kingdom of Tibet.

In her book *Magic and Mystery in Tibet*, David-Néel describes how she embarked on trying to create her own tulpa, in the guise of a kind, rotund medieval monk. Over a period of months, she imagined this character, giving it a history, a personality and motivations. It initially appeared in her mind's eye and then in her peripheral vision as an element of the world outside her immediate control. At first there was nothing problematic about this:

I shut myself in *tsams* [seclusion] and proceeded to perform the prescribed concentration of thought and other rites. After a few months the phantom monk was formed. He became a kind of guest, living in my apartment. I then broke my seclusion and started for a tour, with my servants and tents. The monk included himself in the party. Though I lived in the open, riding on horseback for miles each day, the illusion persisted. It was not necessary for me to think of him to make him appear. The phantom performed various actions of the kind that are natural to travellers and that I had not commanded. For instance, he walked, stopped, looked around him. The illusion was mostly visual, but sometimes I felt as if a robe was lightly rubbing against me, and once a hand seemed to touch my shoulder.[10]

But then things began to change. The figure became leaner and more malevolent. It also began to show a greater degree of independence from her. She realized that she had created something dangerous. It took her more than six months to reabsorb the entity back into her imagination.

Of course, the experiences of David-Néel took place many years ago and in a distant land. We now inhabit a modern, globalized world, where such things simply cannot happen. Or can they?

My research for a previous book on JB Priestley, the British playwright and author, nurtured a friendship between myself and the British theatre producer Braham Murray. We used to meet regularly for lunch in a small Greek restaurant in north London, where we would chat for hours about subjects of mutual interest. Then, one day, out of the blue, Braham announced to me that he knew that non-human, non-physical entities existed and that these beings could be created by the will of a magician. Intrigued, I asked to hear more.

Braham described to me how, one afternoon in 1969, he found himself killing time wandering in and out of the second-hand bookshops around Charing Cross Road on the edge of the London theatre district. He found himself in Cecil Court and a curious bookstore caught his attention (the famous Watkins mind-body-spirit and esoterica shop). On entering, he found it contained a cornucopia of books on esoterical matters. After a wonderful hour of browsing, he decided to purchase a copy of Volume Five of CG Jung's *Symbols of Transformation*. Back home he began reading Jung's work and was immediately fascinated. Later that evening he had a phone call from one of his theatre associates, Casper Wrede, a Finnish baron who had worked with Murray in setting up the Royal Exchange Theatre in Manchester. Wrede told him that the next day, his mentor, Norwegian aristocrat Armund Hohningstadt, was flying into London from Oslo, and he asked if Braham could kindly pick him up from the airport. Although Braham had never met this mysterious person, he knew a great deal about him by reputation. Hohningstadt was known to have a formidable intellect and a keen interest in folklore and the occult. After his chance introduction to Jung that afternoon, Murray felt this imminent meeting was portentous.

Over the next few days Hohningstadt put Braham Murray through an intellectual journey. They discussed all manner of subjects, but mostly revolving around myths and legends. Then one evening Braham asked Hohningstadt about the symbolism of Beauty and the Beast and whether the story could be traced back to the ancient Greek myth of Cupid and Psyche. They then discussed the archetype of the beast in man. They agreed that this was rampant during the Nazi period in Germany, and that the German people had collectively created a monster, a national Egregorial whose character was manifest in the atrocities of the Third Reich. Braham then asked Hohningstadt, "What was the beast?"

When he told me what happened next, Braham sent a shiver up my spine. This is how he tells the story in his autobiography, *The Worst It Can Be Is A Disaster*:

> We were sitting at a table which was against the wall of the kitchen. He was at one end, I was in the middle facing him, the chair at the end was empty. His reply to my question was, "It's over there." The empty chair was now occupied by a creature which was constantly metamorphosing between an ancient woman with Medusa-like snakes for hair and a wizened old man. The other world was in my kitchen, as real as anybody I had ever met.[11]

Braham then explained to me that what he had seen that evening was totally real, but that it had also been created out of thin air by Hohningstadt. He added that from that moment his understanding of what was real and what was not had been totally shattered.

If I am correct in my view that all encounters with non-human entities are, in a real sense, mind-created, then it is reasonable to suggest that any popular belief system, influencing the assumptions and perceptions of large numbers of people, can create collective Egregorials that can manifest powerfully within the Kenoma, being drawn over from the information-laden Pleroma.

According to the respected authority on Western spiritual traditions Mark Stavish, Egregorials can be created by an individual, in which case they are perceived as individual entities; or they can be collectively brought into being by groups who share the same belief system. In the latter case, the Egregorial becomes a manifestation of a collective mind, similar to Plato's concept of the Forms. It becomes real for those who believe in it. This can happen with any abstracted, anthropomorphized concept such as peace, war, love, wealth, nation or tribe – as well as, more significantly, the most powerful of all collective belief systems, religion.

We will now turn our attention to how religious archetypes can manifest into the Kenoma as powerful, emotionally charged images that can literally change history.

CHAPTER 6
RELIGIOUS EGREGORIALS: VIRGINS AND ANGELS

There is a distinct overlap between religion and mysticism. Indeed, many religions are, at heart, mystical. All religions have their own mystical traditions. The scope of this topic is vast, and rather than attempt a wide-ranging overview I have decided to focus on one aspect to allow more depth. Hence, my subject here is Roman Catholicism, and the appearances of an entity, or a number of entities, that have been collectively interpreted as being manifestations of the Blessed Virgin Mary (BVM), the Mother of Jesus.

In 431 CE the leaders of the Christian Church met in Ephesus on the Aegean coast of Asia Minor to declare that Mary, Mother of Jesus, was *Theotokos*, the Greek name for "one who gave birth to God". However, a great deal of the iconography of the Theotokos was based upon the much earlier tradition of the Egyptian Goddess Isis. It is also more than coincidence that Ephesus was the home to another goddess-cult, that of Artemis, a virgin who protected mothers and children. This tradition was in turn based on the ancient cult of Cybele, which has been traced back to at least 6000 BCE. In effect, the Christian Blessed Virgin Mary seems to have been a redefinition of a much older entity.

Visions of the Virgin have been reported since at least the 3rd century CE. The first to be reported with any detailed information dates back to 1061, when a series of encounters took place in Walsingham in Norfolk in eastern England. In the 13th century Caesarius of Heisterbach, a German prior, in his *Dialogus Miraculorum* (Dialogue of Miracles) itemized 64 separate encounters with the Virgin that had been experienced by monks of his own order, the Cistercians. This offers convincing evidence that as an archetypal figure the image of the Virgin Mary is extremely powerful.

As the Catholic faith evolved through the centuries, visionary experiences continued, right into the Industrial Age. The most famous encounter with a figure of the Virgin took place in 1858 in the small mountain settlement of Lourdes in the French Pyrenees.

You will recall that many ancient encounters with Egregorials took place in the gloom or darkness of caves or grottoes. Sightings of the Virgin tend to follow the same pattern. The location in this case was the cave of Massabielle, just outside Lourdes itself.

The cave is on the left bank of the river Gave, a short walk from the town. This had long been identified as the haunt of the *feen* (fairies) popularly known as the "white ladies". Even today the grotto is locally known as the Fairy Cave.

The person who had the experience was a 14-year-old girl named Bernadette Soubirous. Her story has many parallels with UFO abductions and encounters with the Fay. On 11 February 1858, Bernadette was collecting firewood with her sister Toinette and their friend Jeanne Abadie. She lost contact with the other two, who had crossed a stream ahead of her. She then heard a rushing sound and, on turning around to check the source of the noise, saw a white figure standing in the niche of the grotto. When her friends found her, Bernadette was in a deep trance, but she quickly recovered on their arrival. She explained to them what she had seen. After she went back home, her mother, Louise, was worried, believing that what her daughter had encountered was a spirit of the dead. She forbade Bernadette to visit the cave again. By now what had taken place had become a topic of gossip.

In fact, Bernadette was not the first person to have an encounter in this grotto. In a letter to her cousin about this incident, a local woman, Adelaide Monlaur, wrote that some time beforehand a charcoal maker had retreated to the cave from a shower of rain. Sheltering here, he heard moans and cries. Similar noises were heard later by a shepherd. Monlaur added that "a few years ago a fisherman saw a light in the grotto and he was so frightened that he was obliged to flee."

Friends convinced Bernadette to return to the cave. Every time she did so, it was reported that she fell into a deep trance-state, as if possessed. Bernadette tells here of the sight that confronted her:

> … a lady dressed in white, wearing a white dress, a blue girdle and a yellow rose on each foot, the same colour as the chain of her rosary; the beads of the rosary were white. […] From the niche, or rather the dark alcove behind it, came a dazzling light.[1]

It was only during Bernadette's third visit to the cave that the entity spoke to her. It said that the girl should return every day for 15 days. News of this spread quickly, and by the time of the fifteenth appearance, on 4 March, more than 9,000 people were present. A further three appearances were recorded, the last one on 7 April. Officials of the local government then decided that enough was enough and barricaded the cave.

Curiously, there were reports of other peculiar happenings around the cave at that time – including a number of what are now referred to as "satanic" events. These had started during the fourth apparition when Bernadette had heard a cacophony of dark voices rising from the waters of the river. Soon after the visions ended, a young girl named Honorine was at the grotto when she heard voices inside. This happened again the next day, only this time the voices were savage howls, like wild beasts in combat.

From the same period comes this curious report suggesting that the activity around the grotto was far more than an encounter with the Theotokos:

> At the same time, a young man from Lourdes was passing the grotto one day on his way to work before dawn. He crossed himself as he passed the rock, in honour of She who had been present there. Instantly, strange globes of light surrounded him and he felt unable to move. Terrified, he made the Sign of the Cross once more – as he did so, each of the globes of light exploded loudly around him and he was able to leave the place. As this was occurring, he could hear, from within the grotto, maniacal laughter and blasphemies.[2]

There was one final apparition, on Friday 16 July 1858. This was effectively the end of the visions of the Virgin, which stopped as mysteriously as they had begun.

The following year, on 9 October 1859, a curiously similar case took place in Robinsonville, Wisconsin. A 28-year-old woman, Adele Brice (also spelt Brise in some reports), twice saw a luminous white female form, with long wavy yellow hair, wearing a "crown of stars" and a yellow sash across her white dress. As with the Lourdes apparitions, although Adele could see the female figure, others could not. When Adele asked her who she was, the lady replied that she was the "Queen of Heaven" who prays for sinners. Adele reported that this being had appeared between two trees after she had perceived a blinding white light. If this light was as powerful as described, then why did nobody else see anything unusual? This suggests to me that Adele may have experienced a migraine aura or even a temporal lobe seizure. Indeed, after the second encounter, Adele attested that the "heavenly light" surrounding the Lady's body was so bright that she could look directly at her only with difficulty.

This was the first apparition of the Virgin reported in the United States. The Brice family had arrived from Belgium in 1855 and were known to be particularly pious Catholics. Of course, it is possible that these sightings had been influenced by the happenings in Lourdes, but it is important to note that the "Holy Mother" described by Adele had long, golden, wavy hair falling loosely over her shoulders. This is not in any way the typical image of the Virgin found in Catholic iconography.

An intriguing, little-reported Virgin apparition took place in the small town of Pontaine in the Mayenne region of France in January 1871. Twelve-year-old Eugène Barbadette had just heard the news that his half-brother Auguste Friteau, who was serving in the Franco-Prussian war, was safe and well. For some reason he went to the door of the barn where he and his family had been working. Looking out, he noticed the absence of stars over the roof of a nearby house. He then saw the figure of a tall young woman, with an oval face, wearing a deep blue garment on which were scattered haphazardly pentagonal "stars". The figure wore blue shoes and a black veil surmounted with a gold crown, with a red line in its centre. This sight was confirmed by Eugène's brother Joseph but not by his parents. Two small girls who came to the scene saw this figure too, but a third girl did not. Eventually a crowd gathered, and the figure seemed to grow in size until it was covered by a sort of white mist and gradually disappeared. Reports also stated that at one point there was under its feet a sort of tablet, on which writing appeared.

The next fully documented instance is, after Lourdes, the most famous of all. It is the one that has most bearing on our enquiry. This is the vision at Fatima.

One cool spring day in 1916, nine-year-old Lucia Dos Santos and her cousins, Jacinta and Francesco Marto (aged six and eight respectively) were tending sheep on a hillside near the small town of Fatima in central Portugal. At noon, it began to rain and they took shelter in a nearby cave known as the Cova da Iria, or the "Cave of St Irene". This had been the site of a cult for many centuries, surrounding the so-called Senhora da Lapa (Lady of the Rock).

They ate their lunches in the cave and then, after the rain stopped, they ventured outside. A sudden gust of wind shook the treetops and they saw a brilliant, crystal-clear light moving toward them from across the valley. From this light appeared a young man dressed in white. The being told them not to be afraid. He said he was the "angel of peace" and asked them to pray by kneeling down and placing their foreheads on the ground. The angel then went back into the white light and disappeared into the sky. Lucia believed this to be a sacred event and swore her cousins to secrecy. A few months later the angel appeared again at the family well at Arniero. This time the figure announced that it was the "guardian angel" of Portugal. The "angel" visited the children a third time in the autumn of 1916, when it recreated the Eucharist rite and then disappeared.

One year later, on 13 May 1917, the same three children were tending their flock of sheep near the Cova da Iria.

The children found themselves surrounded by a sphere of glowing light, at the centre of which was a little woman with a knee-length skirt. This being told them that she was "from heaven". She said that she would reappear at the same place by the tree on the same day each month for the next five months.

Here again we have an entity appearing at, or near, a cave. When the children had their first encounter, they were actually inside the darkness of a cave for some time, waiting for the rain to stop. We shall explore later a possible explanation why dark, dank locations such as caves have facilitated such experiences for millennia.

On the children's second visit, on 13 June, they were accompanied by around 50 people. Although the crowd saw nothing, the children all reacted at the same time to an invisible presence. It was reported that a sound like the buzzing of bees was heard by some of the witnesses. At the end of the visitation, all of those present heard an explosion and saw a small white cloud appear next to a tree before fading away.

Similar phenomena were reported during the third visitation on 13 July. The crowds had by now increased to over 4,000 and a significant number of these reported buzzing or humming sounds and another explosion and the subsequent reappearance of the small cloud next to a tree.

By now the events in Fatima had become big news. Expectations regarding the 13 August visitation were so great that 18,000 were there to witness the next set of miracles. Sadly, the children were not present. They had been kidnapped by a local official who was concerned that events were getting out of hand. In their absence there was a clap of thunder and the white cloud by the tree made another appearance. Various light-related phenomena were reported, including rainbow effects and flowers seemingly falling from the sky.

The 13 September event was witnessed by a crowd of around 30,000, including a number of sceptics who had turned up to see for themselves how gullible people can be. Two of these were Catholic priests. The priests were shocked to witness a globe of light slowly move down the valley from east to west and settle near the children (no longer under detention). The children were then seen conversing with their invisible friend. The body of light then rose into the sky and disappeared into the glow of the sun.

Everything was now set up for the final, 13 October event. Somewhere in the region of 70,000 people were now crowded together, expecting to witness something extraordinary. They were not disappointed.

At noon there was a huge flash of light, followed by what has now become known as the "Miracle of the Sun". It was reported that the midday sun suddenly appeared like a silver disc and then began to rotate, dance and whirl like a pinwheel with crimson streamers flaring out from the rim. It then zigzagged across the sky for a few moments before returning to its normal, seemingly static, position in the sky.[3]

One of the most intriguing perceptions that links all the altered states of consciousness surrounding encounters with the unknown is the sound of buzzing or whirring. This is reported in OBEs, NDEs, lucid dreaming, UFO encounters and, as we shall soon discover, during psychedelic hallucinations facilitated by a substance termed dimethyltryptamine (DMT). The presence of this aural aspect in visions of the Virgin helps us to see such experiences in their true perspective.

In all the above cases involving children, these young subjects were fervent believers in the truth of Catholic doctrine. They would have been immersed in the faith almost continually. One cannot help wondering if their belief was so strong that they in some way created the apparitions. Now, even though only the children actually claimed to have seen the Lady, hundreds of others witnessed related effects such as the Miracle of the Sun. Could it be that these effects were created by the intense anticipation of the crowds? Unable to see the Virgin, perhaps their psychic need for a spiritual experience enabled them to see something else to reinforce their faith? The question needs to be restated in general terms: can the human mind create Egregorials and allied phenomenon by simply willing them to be? The answer, as we shall see, appears to be yes.

CHAPTER 7
ENTITIES OF MIND POWER

Some of the Egregorials we have examined have existed independently of the human minds encountering them. They show their own motivations; and in many cases their actions run on a different track from those of their human associates, even though they may reflect the belief systems of the cultures in which they appear. It is now time to look at a group of entities that perhaps can be more confidently judged as "mind-created" – though not necessarily in the most obvious ways.

The Ouija experiment
In 1972 one of the most fascinating experiments ever conducted took place. The idea was to create a mind-manifested entity that owed its existence to nothing other than the human imagination.

Members of the Toronto Society for Psychical Research, under the leadership of Iris Owen, had long been intrigued by how ouija sessions work. They wondered if in some way the participants unconsciously create their own self-generated narratives together as the glass moves from letter to letter. To test this possibility, they decided to agree collectively on the life story of a totally fictional historical character.[1]

Owen's group called the entity Philip Aylesford. They gave Philip a whole biography. He was a rich, powerful man who lived in Diddington Manor in England. He had committed suicide in 1654 after an affair with a gypsy girl. Initially, the group was not successful in making contact with this fictitious figure. For more than a year the group meditated on him in vain. Then they decided on a different approach. Instead of serious meditation in atmospheric lighting, they sat around the table in bright light in a deliberately frivolous mood. This, curiously, seemed to work. Much to the group's surprise, the table began to vibrate. Then there was a loud rap. One of the group asked if this was Philip, and a single loud rap gave them an answer. Contact had been made. In the time-tested code of one rap for yes and two raps for no, a rudimentary form of communication was facilitated. Things then took a turn toward the seriously strange. At one point, the table began to move when no one was touching it. It is important to stress that the group were not spiritualists but objectively minded researchers. Indeed, when the table first moved, they believed that one or more of their number were playing around. In a TV interview the group leader, Iris Owen, stated afterwards that so great was the suspicion of cheating that the group had watched each other "like hawks".

Owen explained that repetitive singing seemed to facilitate the effects. In the studio the group was able to recreate the rappings, even though it was clear no one was directly responsible for making these noises.

The experiment, devised by Iris Owen's husband, mathematician ARG Owen, Director of the Toronto Society for Psychical Research, was overseen by psychologist Dr Joel Whitton. On TV Whitton argued that the group had attained a "child-like creativity", facilitated by playfulness, repetitive singing and humour. The orthodox adult mindset, the idea that "this cannot be done", had been set aside. For me this is of great significance.

At that time a psychological theory first proposed by Eric Berne was popular. Transactional Analysis argued that we can adopt one of three "ego states" in our "transactions" with others. These are "Adult", "Child" and "Parent". Whitton suggested that the group collectively adopted a "Child" ego state. I would argue that the entity they conjured is, in fact, a child-Egregorial. The Adult and Parent states, which are predominantly left-brain-generated, can give way at times to a right-brain, child-like propensity. This is infectious. The whole group entered a Child ego-state and, in doing so, opened up the channels that, in childhood, create what Michael Hallowell calls non-corporeal companions (NCCs), or "imaginary friends", something we shall discuss later.

Of course, this gesture toward an explanation in fact explains nothing. How can a collective mindset, embodying an Egregorial, create physical effects in the external world, such as rappings and table turning? In the TV programme Whitton's expert opinion is conveyed with an air of authority that lends him scientific credibility. However, what exactly does he mean when he states that the participants regressed into a child-like state as a form of "subconscious defence mechanism"? A defence mechanism against what? They were not under any form of psychological attack. In fact, they were, by their own admission, feeling very relaxed, telling jokes, singing songs and feeling quite happy.

The "table turning" is particularly intriguing. When the team initially failed to manifest anything of interest, British psychologist Kenneth J Batcheldor suggested they try to reproduce the "table turning" techniques of 19th-century spiritualists. He felt this approach might overcome any residual scepticism in the team, something he suspected was hindering the development of the "entity". In a later interview Joel Whitton explained that in order to see if any of the group was actually pushing or pulling the table in some way, the organizers placed paper "doilies" under the hands of the participants. If they then attempted to push the table, the doilies would simply slide across the surface. This proved that the table movements "were not caused by anybody pushing it". It was also clear from videotapes taken at the time that the group were not using their knees to raise the table. In any case, why would they? They were objective experimenters, not mediums or other occult practitioners trying to prove that they had psychic skills or an ability to communicate with the deceased.

But the question then must be asked: if there was no physical involvement of the participants in the movement of the table (either conscious or subconscious), how could the group be in any way responsible for the table tipping? (It responded in time when the group sang songs together.)

In his book *The Black Arts* (1967) author Richard Cavendish argues that entities evoked by magical rituals may be more than simple hallucinations or wishful thinking on the part of the magician.[2]

Although some manifestations may result from hallucinations, or sometimes deliberate deception, occultists believe that this is not always the case. They say that self-intoxicating procedures are necessary because the spirit is not part of the normal, everyday world and so cannot be experienced in normal states of mind. When prompted to manifest itself out of the magician's imagination, it is a real force. Either it exists independently of the magician, and if so is no more imaginary than electricity or gravity; or it is manifested from *within* the magician, in which case it may be more akin to the forces of ambition, pride or desire which we recognize in ourselves. We can only speculate which kind of reality it possesses. An abnormal state of mind does not necessarily deal in *un*realities. It is only from a conventional, everyday perspective that we can afford to dismiss mind-generated phenomena as illusory. In any case, when things are seen, heard or felt by reliable witnesses, it is reasonable to accept their reality.

Cavendish's suggestion that the human mind can bring about the existence of independent entities by the act of thought alone is in keeping with the principles of quantum physics. A cornerstone of this modern science shows that, at the quantum level, the act of observation can create the physical world. We shall focus in more details on the implications of this idea later.

The whole concept of mind-created entities is far more complex than any simple explanation involving a materialist-reductionist dismissal or a spiritualist's blind belief. Philip seems actually to have come to life – or life-after-death – in a way our rational minds cannot fully comprehend.

A scientific paper published in April 2019 suggested that the actual location of this kind of super-creative ability may be a part of the brain known as the "dorsomedial default network". This consists of a group of interconnected brain regions, including the medial prefrontal cortex, the posterior cingulate cortex, the angular gyrus and the hippocampus. This area of the brain is particularly powerful when it comes to visualization. The team, led by Meghan Meyer, Assistant Professor of Psychological and Brain Science at Dartmouth College, New Hampshire, set out to discover whether creative people have stronger "imagination muscles" than non-creative people.

To see these imagination muscles in action, they asked 27 creative types and 26 control participants to go through simulation tasks while lying in a functional magnetic resonance imaging (fMRI) scanner. Brain activity of the creative adepts and controls was similar when imagining future events over the next 24 hours; however, to the researchers' surprise, the creative group alone engaged the dorsomedial default network when imagining events further into the future.

The dorsomedial default network was not active at all among the control group; and yet, even at rest, this area of the brain was active for the creative group.[3]

I cannot help wondering if it is this creative facility that was accessed by the Toronto team and assisted in the creation of Philip.

A type of group-think

It seems that human consciousness, specifically when acting collectively, as a group-consciousness, can create something both greater than, and external to, the individuals involved.

There is evidence that the entity Philip "created" by the Toronto group showed knowledge and skills greater than those available to the group members, either individually and collectively. In relation to this idea, parapsychologist Scott Rogo has suggested that groups can bring into existence something greater than its individual members:

> There is another psychological factor which comes into play during group-PK practices [...] group-PK effects are often directed by a collective mind created by the sitters. By joining forces, several people may actually form some sort of semiautonomous will or mind that directs the PK. Now this "entity" is not "owned" by or dependent upon any single group member. It is, on the contrary, semi-independent of all of them. A PK group, therefore, can overcome ownership inhibition because the PK is really being architectured by an ego-alien personality.[4]

What Rogo means by PK is a phenomenon known as "psychokinesis". This is an ability that certain people allegedly exhibit whereby they can move objects or influence physical systems without direct contact. Rogo, who built a reputation on evaluating the claims of PK, until his death in 1990 was convinced that such an ability was innate in all human beings. In the passage quoted above he argues for a form of "collective-PK" in which a group of like-minded individuals can focus their intention to create an alien and non-human intelligence that has a form of independence from its creators. However, this independence comes at a cost: in order to continue to exist, the entity needs sustenance in the same way a living animal needs food and water to stay alive. For such beings, sustenance comes from the energy generated by powerful human emotions such as fear, hate and love.

One of the most intriguing applications of this hypothesis is presented by American parapsychology researcher Paul Eno. In his book *Turning Home: God, Ghosts and Human Destiny,* former Roman Catholic priest Eno argues that many of the "entities" encountered during altered states of consciousness, hauntings and associated experiences are actually psychic vampires that feed on strong emotions.

Eno's argument is a particularly elegant one, and worth serious consideration. He observes that the oldest tales of vampires found in various cultural and folk traditions from around the world describe not blood-suckers but ghosts who suck life out of the living. He then goes on to argue that these entities may masquerade as demons or the ghosts of those once alive, but this is not their true identity. They have the ability to manipulate the perceptions of human beings to appear in whatever guise is acceptable to a particular culture or set of circumstances. This is similar to my own concept of an Egregorial, a created entity that seems to exist in the three-dimensional space surrounding us but is in fact an elemental creation of the mind – though one with true existence, a reality that is more than illusory.

Eno argues that many of these Egregorials are parasites that feed on life energy, generated by extreme human emotions such as fear or hate. These parasites, he believes, occur in a number of different species and all have subtly different motivations. What they have in common is the need to generate emotions in their human prey to provide them with sustenance. To differentiate Eno's entities I will, from now on, use the term Parasite with a capital initial, as he does.

Eno points out that, although human beings are carbon-based life forms, his experiences with these parasitic entities (and he has had many of them) suggest that their existence may be based on plasma. He writes:

Most Parasites even look like plasma in one form or another, both in photographs and on the rare occasions I see them with the naked eye. Some species appear smoky, either light or dark. Others look very bright, almost like bolts of lightning. Still other kinds appear as shadowy figures, some nearly solid. Some can be quite disconcertingly solid, though this is rare.[5]

This is thought-provoking. You will recall that during our review of the djinn (p42) we discovered that according to Islamic teachings these entities were created out of "smokeless fire". Could this be interpreted as plasma?

Eno observes that when a Parasite manages to take over the thought processes of a large number of people, they can generate huge amounts of "food" for the entity. He suggests that this may be what takes place when nations are taken over by extremist political philosophies such as National Socialism. The amount of terror and fear that such regimes can generate is incalculable.

It seems reasonable to conclude that ghosts and associated phenomena, just like the visions of the Virgin and of angels within a Catholic context discussed in the last chapter, are another variation on our egregorial model. The question that we must now ask is whether these manifestations are human. If ghosts are the spirits of departed human beings, then they must be humans in a non-embodied form. If they are not, then what exactly are they? Answers to this question may be sought in our attempts to make contact with these disembodied entities and open up direct communication. We will now turn our attention to this sensitive area of mediumship.

CHAPTER 8

MESSAGES FROM SPIRIT AND ALIEN REALMS

Attempts to communicate with spirits have taken place throughout history. We have already discussed in some detail the attempts made by magicians and other occultists. But the premise of these approaches was that the entities involved were non-human. The idea of communication with the dead, although attempted throughout the centuries, became popular only in the early 19th century with the growth of spiritualism. However, some attempts to communicate with the "dead" appear more like egregorial engagements than discussions with the departed. One such example is the curious case of Imperator and Rector in the late 19th century.

Imperator and Rector

In early April 1872 a London-based Anglican priest, William Stainton Moses, had an experience that was to change totally his belief that mediumship and spirit communication were, as he had termed them, the "dreariest twaddle". He had been invited by a friend, Mrs Speer, to attend a séance led by a very popular medium, Lottie Fowler. In this sitting Moses was given some powerful evidence that a recently deceased friend was communicating from somewhere beyond our everyday, living world. Moses was intrigued and soon began his own investigation into mediumship. Much to his surprise, he discovered that he himself had mediumistic abilities. Later, in 1882, Moses became one of the founder members of the Society for Psychical Research (SPR).

Moses discovered he could fall into a trance state, witnessing physical effects that would also be seen by the other members of the circle. These included loud rapping noises, music and, of particular significance (as we shall see later), floating globes of light that moved rapidly around the room.

The sounds heard in these sessions are also significant. One type that was regularly heard was what the group called the "fairy bells". This was a sound similar to that made when drinking glasses are struck lightly with a metal implement. This was never heard as a tune, just a series of tones.

The physical manifestations, involving floating lights, sounds and smells, were regularly accompanied by "communications". The sources of these identified themselves as "spirits" but, as Moses himself states in his book *Spirit Teachings*, the actual identity of these entities remains unknown. They may have called themselves "spirits" because that is what he called them when they first manifested. For the purposes of this discussion I prefer to use the term "entities", which reflects more accurately their mysterious nature.

Provided that Moses was not a fake, the entities were able to manipulate physical objects in everyday reality. They could also create electromagnetic effects such as floating lights. Moreover, they had the ability to use Moses' vocal cords to communicate information. However, his main form of contact with them was through something known as passive, or automatic, writing. In this process, the medium holds a pen or pencil and then waits for something to take over his or her hand; when this happens, the hand writes down messages. These written communications took an interesting turn when, in March 1873, one specific entity started signing off the messages as the "Doctor" or the "Teacher".[1]

Soon more spirits came through, but eventually one entity started to communicate on behalf of the rest. This one signed itself "Rector". Soon a second group, headed by a grandly named being calling itself "Imperator", also appeared. An example of the power and dignity (even pomposity) of these announcements can be gleaned from this transcript recorded by Dr Stanhope Speer, husband of the woman who first introduced Moses to spiritualism:

> I, myself, Imperator Servus Dei, am the chief of a band of forty-nine spirits, the presiding and controlling spirit, under whose guidance and direction the others work [...] I am come from the seventh sphere to work out the will of the Almighty; and, when my work is complete, I shall return to those spheres of bliss from which none returns again to earth. But this will not be till the medium's work on earth is finished, and his mission on earth exchanged for a wider one in the spheres.[2]

What is fascinating about these communications is the suggestion of concerted effort by an organized group of entities to send messages from an alternative universe to this one. Imperator explains that he is the leader of the group, with other entities taking on specific areas of responsibility to facilitate communication.

Rector is his deputy and lieutenant, while the role of the Doctor is to guide the pen of the receiving medium. In other words, Imperator, or occasionally Rector, would dictate information to the Doctor who would then take over the medium's hand. In this way messages are transferred from the "Seventh Sphere" to our own world. Also involved is a team of four beings called the "Guardians". In total the team consists of seven entities. This team of seven is part of a much larger group responsible for guiding life on Earth.

In one communication, Imperator attempts to explain to his human associates how his team is able to use their advanced knowledge of science to communicate across the dimensions:

We have a higher form of what is known to you as electricity, and it is by that means we are enabled to manifest, and that Mentor shows his globe of light. He brings with him the nucleus, as we told you.[3]

"Mentor" is a member of the "band of 49 spirits" who seem to have been tasked with designing the process by which communication channels could be opened. Of particular interest here is the use of the term "nucleus". The word was not to become associated with any form of physics until May 1911 when it was used by Ernest Rutherford to describe the centre of the atom. Although the term "nucleus" had first been used in 1831 by Scottish botanist Robert Brown, this was in relation to plant cells, not physics. Imperator's deployment of this terminology is remarkable, suggesting a knowledge of physics far in advance of the 1870s.

In *More Spiritual Teachings* Moses describes how he was able to travel into the world of Imperator and the 49 spirits. This is similar to many classic cases of hypnagogia, out-of-body and shamanic experiences and, as we shall discover later, DMT (facilitated altered states of consciousness, as described in my previous book, *Opening the Doors of Perception*).

Moses describes what happened when he went to bed one evening. As he was lying there, he heard the "fairy bells" and saw around his bed the globes of light. He then lost consciousness to find himself standing next to a large lake surrounded by verdant hills. As he made his way along the shore, he saw, walking toward him, a figure dressed in a white robe. As he got closer he could see that the figure was a bearded man and that the robe was of a peculiar pearly whiteness. Moses immediately knew that this person was "Mentor". Clearly expecting him, Mentor announced that they were in "Spirit-Land" and that he needed to follow him. Moses was then led to a beautiful villa where he met an even more imposing white-robed figure. By some form of intuition, he knew that this was Imperator. He again mentions how stunningly white Imperator's robes were, "composed of dewdrops, lit by the morning sun."[4] He then met up with the other members of the "49 spirits", all dressed in similarly white robes. He then found himself back in this reality, as if awaking from a dream, but one far more real than waking life. From this experience he concluded that the spirit world is all around us: it is just that our eyes are not opened enough to perceive it.

It may be significant that during some of his automatic-writing episodes Moses experienced a form of out-of-body experience. In another intriguing passage in *More Spirit Teachings*, he states that he viewed his body from a position beside himself. He notes that he could also see the whole room, everything material in it being "shadowy", a ghostly reflection of the "spiritual world" that has made itself felt here.[5] He then notes that his associates Rector, Imperator and several of the other "49" were in the room watching what was happening. This again convinces Moses that both worlds, the earthly and the spiritual, overlap. What is really intriguing is his observation of the entities "passing in and out", as if viewing the experiment for a few minutes, then going back to the spirit land to do other things. He also points out that his hand, which, you will recall, he was viewing from an out-of-body state, was "charged" by a bluish light.

One of the most intriguing references in Moses' narrative is to the existence of what he terms "imposter spirits". He is told that these antagonistic entities, known as the "adversaries", can be exceedingly dangerous.

In early February 1882 Sir William Barrett, a professor of physics at the Royal College of Science, Dublin, initiated a meeting of scientists, philosophers and spiritualists to discuss how the scientific method could be applied to mediumship. From this meeting was created the organization known as the Society for Psychical Research (SPR). A few weeks later, on 20 February 1882, the society was formally constituted under the presidency of Henry Sidgwick, a Cambridge University professor of classics. The council consisted of 18 members, including Barrett himself, a classical scholar named Edmund Gurney, the outspoken sceptic Frank Podmore, an eminent classical scholar called FWH Myers and Stainton Moses himself.

Given Moses' involvement, it comes as no surprise that one of the first investigations of the SPR focused on his communications with spirit entities. This work was undertaken by FWH Myers. After a thorough investigation, Myers came to the conclusion that the phenomena were genuine. That they

> … were not produced fraudulently by Dr Speer or other sitters. […] I regard as proved both by moral considerations and by the fact that they were constantly reported as occurring when Mr Moses was alone. That Mr Moses should have himself fraudulently produced them I regard as both morally and physically incredible. That he should have prepared and produced them in a state of trance I regard both as physically incredible and also as entirely inconsistent with the tenor both of his own reports and those of his friends. I therefore regard the reported phenomena as having actually occurred in a genuinely supernormal manner.[6]

Moses died in 1892, but in an intriguing development the Imperator group made another attempt at communication with our own plane of existence three years later, this time using Mrs Piper, a famous psychic of the time, as their chosen medium. Right from the start of their involvement with Mrs Piper, Imperator and his associates, Rector and the Doctor, took steps to make it clear that they were the same entities that had communicated with, and through, Stainton Moses.

Were they in fact the same group? There is strong evidence to suggest not. On occasions the new group showed remarkable ignorance about the announcements of the earlier one. However, there is evidence that the first group did keep trying to come through – for example, in messages channelled by a medium named Minnie M Soule and, in the 1920s, in the automatic scripts of another sensitive, Gwendolyn Kelley Hack. But what was certain was that this form of communication was a quite different type of information exchange than was typical of standard mediumship. The messages given were designed to assist and improve the whole of humankind rather than conveying intensely personal insights to the relatives of someone deceased.

From other worlds: Scole

From the 1950s onwards there has been a series of "communications" from entities claiming to represent extraterrestrial civilizations keen to help humankind in a similar way to that outlined by Imperator and Rector. Is it possible that the phenomenon has simply evolved to reflect how our society has advanced and become more and more technological in its approach?

Scole, a village in the mostly rural county of Norfolk in eastern England, in the 1990s presented dramatic evidence that new forms of communication were being developed by those on the "other side". Although easily accessible from London, Norfolk has a reputation for sleepy tranquillity tinged with a deep otherworldliness. It is therefore not surprising that this part of East Anglia played host to a series of strange psychic experiments from 1993 to 1998. The initial plan followed by a small group of psychic investigators was to use standard mediumship to open up communication with the spirit world, but it soon became clear that the "entities" that manifested were keen to try new methods – ones more appropriate to the 21st century that was about to dawn than to a century already long past, the 19th.

The Scole team, led by retired Royal Air Force pilot Robin Foy, used trance mediums Diana and Alan Bylett as the facilitators. The intention was to set up a perfect environment for spirit communication. To their surprise, the team found themselves seemingly in contact with an organized group of individuals who were keen to advance communications. Each of the entities who communicated through the Byletts had specific personalities and each one identified itself by name. One who called itself "Manu" seemed to be the leader; another, "Emily Bradshaw", was "Mistress of Ceremonies". Other spirit beings included a jovial Irishman named Patrick, an Indian named Raji and a cultured Englishman, Edward. The entities gave specific instructions as to what should be placed where in the séance room, nicknamed the "Scole Hole".

Physical manifestations soon took place, such as the materialization of various "apports", objects believed to appear in this world having been sent from another, together with images appearing on 35mm film placed in sealed and seemingly tamper-proof containers. One apport was a newspaper from 1944 that appeared as if from nowhere and in absolute pristine condition. Later tests were to show that the paper itself, and the printing ink used in its production, were authentic for the period.

News of what was taking place at Scole soon spread. Investigators from the Society for Psychical Research came to witness the events, three of these – Montague Keen, Arthur Ellison and David Fontana – subsequently wrote a book about their findings. All seemed convinced that something significant had happened.[7]

Other independent researchers also made their way to the house. In September 1996 the present President of the Scottish Society for Psychical Research (SSPR), Nick Kyle, his wife Sarah and two other SSPR members sat with the Scole team. This group consisted of a head of computer services; a qualified hypnotherapist; a training manager for a national

UK company; and two teachers, one with a research degree. This group had been stimulated to request a sitting with the Scole team because they were collectively frustrated about an ongoing lack of hard evidence in support of medium-facilitated communications. At the first session the Scottish group were presented with phenomena that startled them. These included a series of lights moving responsively around the room and in doing so illuminating their immediate surroundings. Kyle was later to describe how the lights entered:

> … solid objects such as a crystal which glowed, or passing through the table, or entering the torsos of participants, including Sarah! I had never seen "energy lights" before. Now we knew what they looked like and they partially illumined their surroundings as they sped around at high speeds. Even if David Copperfield [a well-known TV magician] himself could have faked such a light show, he could not have tickled the inside of my wife's ribcage![8]

All this is uncannily similar to the phenomena described by Stainton Moses and his team a century before. Is this merely coincidence or can it be seen as evidence of a comparable *modus operandi*?

Kyle and his associates were perplexed by what they witnessed. They returned six months later and were presented with even more powerful happenings. Lights again were manifest, but this time in groups of three linked by white-blue beams. Kyle observed from one of these "hovering triangular wedges" several tiny searchlight-like beams stretching out to illuminate the table as if exploring it. Then things became strange indeed:

> Two slightly yellow shapes were perplexing and are difficult to describe. One appeared as if you were looking through an illuminated lens down a tiny kaleidoscope at another illuminated lens, giving a clear impression of

depth. The other, larger tube pointed toward me briefly and I saw within it a tiny outstretched hand, as if I could see from the tips of the fingers down the length of a small forearm. The hand seemed feminine and, as it passed me, another hand was visible beside it in a cupping action.[9]

These events convinced Kyle and his associates that what they had witnessed at Scole was something paranormal. In one of his letters to me Kyle stated categorically that, although a strong sceptic, he felt that "What I witnessed at Scole has left me no longer at ease in the old dispensation of traditional physical mediumship. I have seen what is possible using new methods of communication and it has fuelled my interest ever since."[10]

These "new methods of communication" include the use of modern technology to facilitate information-transfer between worlds. No longer are we dependent upon physical or mental mediumship. In the same way that telephony and, in recent years, web-based tools such as Skype have replaced written and face-to-face verbal communication, so it is that telephones, radios and TVs have become a preferred form of "spirit" contact.

One of the major experiments that took place at Scole involved a video camera and a "double psychomanteum". This device was suggested by one of the entities. It consisted of two mirrors. One was placed behind the video camera so it could capture and reflect the circle of light emanating from the viewfinder back toward the second mirror situated at the front of the video camera. This was supposed, by processes unclear, to create a doorway between this world and that of the entities. In this respect, I cannot help being reminded of the Alam al-Mithal of the Persian Sufis, the "gateway" between the Molk and the Malakut, between the Kenoma and the Pleroma. Here we have an old idea applied to new technology.

Because this process also involved the use of mirrors, the team nicknamed it "Project Alice", in reference to Lewis Carroll's *Alice through the Looking-glass*. To the surprise of the team, a visual image came though, a non-human face:

> Gradually the line turned sideways and the square screen came into view, now seen from the front. The amazing thing was that as the screen rotated, it had an image on it. This was a very clear view of an "animated interdimensional friend" whose features to say the least were not exactly our own. This friend has been named "Blue".[11]

The visual characteristics of Blue suggest that this entity was in some way related to much of the egregorial imagery we have discussed in our journey through time. Blue has large black eyes, a tiny nose and a non-existent mouth. This echoes the account of one of Evans-Wentz's Irish interviewees from 1914, when she encountered a giant fairy-creature with eyes like "two dark caverns". And what about the 10,000-year-old Indian cave paintings at Gotitola, with their big-eyed "rohela people" (see p12)? Or the large-eyed entities depicted on the "Bridge Scene" in South Africa's Junction Shelter painted in the Upper Paleolithic (p13)? Or finally, my mother's nocturnal visitor described in my Prologue (p1). Also, take out the large black eyes and focus on the overall face shape, tiny nose and virtually non-existent mouth and you have Aleister Crowley's Lam looking back at you.

Is this all just coincidence? A cultural memory transmitted somehow from one cultural context to another? Or is it simply that this is one of the most powerful egregorial images that passes through from the Pleroma to the Kenoma?

It seems that the communicators at Scole, and those earlier entities in dialogue with Stainton Moses, are far more than simply dead people trying to make contact with the living. Whatever their true nature, these entities will choose whatever guise is culturally acceptable to their human interlocutors. As technology has advanced and as our collective worldview has changed, so have the Egregorials. They mirror our expectations and fulfil whatever we wish of them. John Dee wanted Archangels, and Archangels is what he got. Stainton Moses wanted the spirits of the dearly departed, and that too is what he got. The Toronto Team knowingly created the fiction of Philip Aylesford and dutifully Philip appeared. Alexandra David-Néel and her Tibetan friends created their friendly monk as a collective thought form and, like Philip, he became independent of them and developed his own will.

This suggests that there is an apparent relationship between Egregorials and human consciousness, both individual and collective. Either they seem to impose themselves upon our consciousness to manifest in the Kenoma or else we project them into the Kenoma from our own subconscious, allowing them to fulfil our greatest hopes and fears.

Since the end of World War II, the world has become a dangerous place, with global destruction just a push-of-a-button away. It is not surprising that we have looked elsewhere for company – to the stars in the hope that we are not alone in our self-referential consciousness and that somewhere out there are creatures like us.

We now reach the final chapter of our review of different types of Egregorials by looking at one of the great mysteries of modern times: UFOs and their supposed pilots.

CHAPTER 9
EXTRATERRESTRIALS AND ABDUCTIONS

Since records have been kept, there have been reports of people being abducted by non-human entities and taken away to alien environments. In ancient Greek mythology the gods were regularly whisking away young women. For example, the abduction of Persephone by the god Hades. In this tale the young woman is taken into the Underworld. While there, she is persuaded to eat four seeds of a pomegranate. In doing so she transgresses against a fundamental rule, and hence is doomed to return to the abode of her divine lover for four months of every year (winter). As we shall discover, partaking of food or drink in the world of the Egregorials is not a good idea.

I would like now to give a small selection of "alien abduction" cases from around the world. These events took place in different cultures and at different time periods. What intrigues me are the consistencies in the reports, suggesting that this is a genuine phenomenon and more than simply hallucination or storytelling.

Alien abductions

Cases where individuals have been taken into the sky by non-human entities have been reported for hundreds of years. The earliest account of what may be considered an alien abduction took place in 1752 in Kazan in Russian central Asia when Mr Yashka encountered a white-clothed stranger who took him on board what was described as a "flying cauldron".[1] Sadly I can find no further details relating to this intriguing incident, but it does show how fairy-like abductions and UFO encounters all come down to interpretation.

In 1897 in St Louis, USA, Joseph Joslin noticed a strange large object on the ground. Next to it was a small humanoid creature that hypnotized him and seemingly abducted him. He was away for three weeks but remembered nothing. This "lost time" is very much a theme of modern encounters, and here we have a case from more than 120 years ago where the same theme is found.

Earlier in our enquiry we discussed the discoveries of 10,000-year-old cave paintings in India depicting what look like alien entities and flying machines. In my research I have discovered a case that took place in 1931 in Andhra Pradesh. A 14-year-old boy was looking after his cattle when he noticed a strange man meditating. The being explained to the boy that he was from another world. A flying object then landed in front of these new friends and the boy entered it. Inside he was introduced to a group of similarly meditating entities. He was then given some fruit to eat and something that looked like a mirror with images on it. He was taken for a number of days and claimed during this time that he was held in a machine in space.

In February 1917 an object shaped like a wash tub landed on the shores of Lake Kankaanlampi in Finland. A local woman, Anni Lattu, was subsequently abducted by a group of small entities that came out of this flying machine.

Over the years alien encounters involving the abduction of individuals have become more prevalent. This may simply be that such encounters are more widely reported in the mass media and abductees are more at ease sharing their strange experiences. Of course, these cases can easily be dismissed as hallucinations, the work of overactive imaginations or simply fabrications. Lack of physical evidence to support such cases supports such a belief. However, in the late 20th century a new variation on the abduction scenario began to be reported. This involved claims that during the abduction the aliens place implants in the bodies of the abductee. The curious factor here is that in the vast majority of the cases the "alien implants" are actually found to be fairly mundane, human-created objects. This suggests that there is a strong psychological element here whereby the actual experience has many parallels with the shamanic travelling dismemberment theme that we have already discussed.

For example, in 1992 a 13-year-old boy, James Basil, had an uncanny experience while he was lying in bed. He stretched out his hand which then came in contact with another hand, not human: it was smooth and lizard-like with curled fingers. He then opened his eyes and saw two aliens standing at the end of his bed. This was the start of a series of encounters with these creatures over a period of years.

In 1997 he discussed his experiences with parapsychologist Dr Susan Blackmore as part of a student project. Blackmore was sure that he was suffering from a form of sleep paralysis. However, he was able to present Blackmore with physical evidence: he claimed that the aliens had implanted a small object in his mouth, and a few weeks later, in another operation, they removed it. For some reason the aliens left the implant with him and he promised he would bring it in for Blackmore to examine. She subsequently saw the object and described it as being 2mm × 3mm in size and a dullish grey colour. Subsequent analysis showed the "implant" to actually be a tooth filling.

There is arguably a curious link between UFO abductions and shamanic initiations. You will recall how dismemberment was a prelude to the shamanic journey (see p17); we also examined how the dismemberment theme was the basis of the Osiris myth of ancient Egypt (p31).

Alien abductions and shamanism

According to Graham Hancock, certain Australian Aboriginal traditions involve supernatural beings placing snakes deep inside the initiate's brain. The process is macabre:

> Their sides are cut open and [...] their internal organs are removed and they are provided with a new set. A snake is put in their heads and their noses are pierced by a magical object (*kupitja*) that will later serve them in curing the sick. These objects are believed to have been made in the mythical Alcheringa times [the "Dreamtime"] by certain very powerful snakes.[2]

Initially here we have the classic shamanic dismemberment theme. It bears repeating that Hancock's example reflects the beliefs of one of the most isolated human communities on Earth, and yet their traditions describe *exactly* the same dismemberment motif shown by other shamanic traditions thousands of miles away across the vast open seas. We know that the indigenous animals in Australia are like no others on the planet, attesting to just how isolated Australia has been over millions of years. How can groups of nomadic hunter-gatherers in the "Red Centre" of Australia echo themes described by Siberian Tungas and the Sami of Finland?

It is evident that the shamanic dismemberment-and-journey theme is a universal human experience, transcending time and space. Many people might assume that such things do not take place in supposedly "sophisticated", scientifically "rational" societies, such as modern-day California. You will recall that earlier, in the Introduction, we encountered the intriguing experiences of Californian artist Myron Dyal. As well as his extraordinary encounters with fairies, leprechauns and elves, Myron also describes a couple of altogether more macabre experiences that are more in keeping with shamanic dismemberment and the bizarre medical "experiments" encountered by UFO abductees.

The first encounter took place at a location he calls the "Place of the Four Stars" in May 1976. What started as being simply an amorphous black figure at the side of him becomes a Minotaur, a creature from mythology, half man, half bull. He fights this creature, kills it and then dismembers it. Then he eats the creature and takes its spirit into himself. Yet again we have shamanic imagery breaking through here – but, remember, these incidents were experienced not in the deep past nor in some remote region of the planet but in a park in San Francisco.

In December 1978 events were to take an even more distinctly shamanic turn. Myron was on his way to meet a business client when he decided to turn off Freeway 405 and visit a statue of the Virgin of Guadalupe in the Holy Cross Cemetery in Culver City. On arriving there, Myron felt as if he was being watched, or even stalked. Now what may be significant here is that the statue was located in a small grotto and next to a waterfall. So we have running water and a small cave – two factors that seem to facilitate otherworldly experiences (see p171). Myron was suddenly transported to a forest where he was surrounded by tall trees. Here he encountered the usual flickering light, but this time it was part of the altered state perceptions, rather than something happening in the Kenoma. He encountered a pack of wolf-like creatures with startlingly red eyes – beings, it turned out, that had been with him since childhood. The creatures then attacked him:

> Then I was overwhelmed by them, consumed. Skin hung from me in tatters, my bones were snapped between their powerful jaws, my skull caved in, my eyes were their appetizer, my heart their entree. It was the episode with the black Minotaur but in reverse. This time, I was being eaten. They chewed great gouts of flesh out of me, then

with quick jerks of their massive canine heads they threw them into the night. Finally, I was no more.[3]

In shamanism, dismemberment is followed by the resurrection of the shaman and an encounter with the divine self, the other that until now has been hidden. This is exactly what happened to Myron. As soon as the horror of attack was over, he was approached by a tall, elderly man with a white beard, dressed in a white robe. According to shamanic beliefs, the proto-shaman is reassembled ready for his future calling. The tall figures performed this restorative function for Myron:

> I was being reborn as a picture is painted, piece by piece, section by section, from the ground up. After my head was restored I was still without features and without an outer dermis. But he was not yet finished with his task. He continued his work of remaking Myron Dyal, slowly but surely, expertly; I had absolute confidence in his ability and knowledge to fulfil his task. He rebuilt me and the new body was glowing with a bluish light, very beautiful to behold, which turned out to be the matrix for the finishing touches, skin, muscles, sinew, each put in its proper place, pulled taut, made smooth.[4]

Those readers familiar with my book *Opening the Doors of Perception* will know that I suggest that Myron's encounters with the egregorial realm were (and they continue to be) facilitated by his temporal lobe epilepsy. It is well known that many shamans throughout history have been selected to follow this path on the basis of their outward behaviours, specifically symptoms of what has become known as the "falling sickness" or the "diviner's disease". Romanian historian-philosopher, and recognized expert on shamanism, Mircea Eliade, has tellingly observed on the links between shamanic experiences and temporal lobe epilepsy: "the only difference between a shaman and an epileptic is that the latter cannot deliberately enter into a trance."[5] It is interesting to compare Eliade's account of typical shamanic dismemberment initiation with Myron describing his encounters with the red-eyed creatures.

Eliade writes:

> The content of these first ecstatic experiences, although comparatively rich, always includes one or more of the following themes: dismemberment of the body, followed by a renewal of the internal organs or viscera; ascent to the sky and dialogue with the gods or spirits; descent to the underworld and conversations with spirits and the souls of dead shamans.[6]

In fact, there are many parallels to be drawn between classic alien abductions and shamanism. Earlier we encountered examples of shamanic beliefs, specifically the shamanic cosmology of non-human entities existing in other worlds that overlap with our own. Such a scenario was described to Evans Wentz by an Irish "seer". This bears repeating:

> The shining beings belong to the mid-world; while the opalescent beings belong to the heaven-world. There are three great worlds which we can see while we are still in the body: the earth-world, mid-world, and heaven-world.'[7]

Remember too that Evans-Wentz concluded that such experiences were not hallucinations but encounters with real entities existing in an alternative reality outside our normal perceptions. Evans-Wentz makes the following observation:

> It is mathematically possible to conceive fourth-dimensional beings, and if they exist it would be impossible in a three-dimensional plane to see them as they really are. Hence the ordinary apparition is non-real as a form, whereas the

beings, which wholly sane and reliable seers claim to see when exercising seership of the highest kind, may be as real to themselves and to the seers as human beings are to us here in this three-dimensional world when we exercise normal vision.[8]

By this, Evens-Wentz is suggesting that the objective appearance of these entities as they are in four-dimensional space is modified when they are perceived in our three-dimensional space. The entities are, in a very real sense, mind-created, but this does not invalidate their objective existence. Their appearance to us is moulded by our personal belief system. They are, in a very literal sense, Egregorials as described earlier in this discussion.

Could it simply be that our interpretations of these encounters have changed over the years and that what were, in the past, interpreted as encounters with the "secret commonwealth" are now regarded as encounters with aliens? These are changes over time, but there are also changes related to location and culture. That encounters with Egregorials are culturally interpreted is self-evident. When encountering something outside our everyday experience, which seemingly contradicts our understanding of how the world works, we will try and place such experiences within our own socially conditioned model of how the world functions. This applies to UFO encounters in the same way as it can apply to religious beliefs or folklore.

It is therefore important to look at UFO encounters as they are perceived and interpreted in non-Western cultures – for example, in the Islamic world.

An Eastern perspective

Earlier we discussed in some detail the Middle Eastern concept of the djinn (see p42). We discovered that these entities are believed to be interdimensional: they exist in a reality that is extremely close to this one and they can, when they wish to, cross over from their reality into ours – in my own terminology from the the Pleroma to the Kenoma.

In my research I came across an intriguing case from Iran in the mid-1970s. This suggests that a direct link can be made between UFO encounters and contact with the mercurial djinn.

In their book *The Truth about Alien Abductions* (1997), Peter Hough and Moyshe Kalman describe in detail an alien abduction encounter that took place in the Iranian village of Ahar, northeast of Tehran, in September 1976. It involved British university lecturer Dr Simon Taylor and an Iranian civil servant identified as "Reza".

The two men had travelled to the village to escape the oppressive summer heat and pollution of Tehran and enjoy a set of walks in the Elburz mountains. After a short drive, they left the car and soon arrived on foot at one of the many climbers' cabins that could be found in the area. Here they spent the night. Some time in the early hours of the morning, the cabin was shaken by some heavy, pounding thumps. The two men ran outside and saw, a short distance away, three men dressed from head to foot in black, carrying torch-like instruments. On approaching them, Simon noticed they had abnormally large black eyes.

What then took place was a series of "telepathic" communications, by which the two walkers were instructed to follow the three men in black along the mountain path that led back to the village of Ahar. After walking for a few hundred feet, Taylor became aware that they were no longer on a path but in some kind of room. Instead of stones and twigs beneath their feet there was an elaborately decorated Persian carpet. The men turned off their torches and the room was illuminated by a soft, white light. It became clear that this "room" was inside some form of flying machine that was rapidly rising into the air. Along one wall was a huge screen that seemingly showed what could be seen outside. They saw the lights of Tehran recede into the distance. What then took place was an amazing journey:

I cannot remember all the places we "visited", but
I distinctly remember fantastic aerial panoramas of London,
New York, Paris and my home city of Birmingham. We
saw deserts and frozen wastes of ice and snow, seas – more
water than I had ever seen in my life! The pictures were
crystal clear and three-dimensional.[9]

After the "journey" had ended, the two men were asked to
leave and suddenly found themselves back on the mountain
path. They discovered that six hours had passed during their
time in the "room". They walked down toward the village in a
daze, and it was only after buying and eating some food that
they discussed their experience. They wondered if it was some
form of shared hallucination brought about by the paraffin
lamps in the cabin. However, they were not convinced by any
such rational explanation.

Dr Taylor never returned to Iran. Even 20 years after the
experience, any thoughts about what had happened to him
brought on violent migraine attacks. But he was still keen
to understand the episode. In 1977 he met with Iranian
Islamic scholar Mustata Chamran in London and took the
opportunity to describe this incident of three years earlier.
Chamran was sure that the beings that Taylor had encountered
that night were not aliens but something far more sinister:
djinn. It is worth pointing out at this point that the Elburz
Mountains are volcanic in origin. Indeed, the highest volcano
in Asia, Damavand, is still active here, with fumaroles near
the summit. The name Damavand means "the mountain from
which smoke and ash arises". The village of Ahar is no more
than 85 kilometres (just over 50 miles) from Damavand, and
the mountain is visible from the village.

In my researches on the subject, I discovered that this
mountain is Mount Meru. Its original name may have been
Divband, "home of the spirits". In 1925 the mountain was
climbed by Swedish explorer Sven Anders Hedin, who was
informed that the mountain was, in fact, home to both

good (*divs*) and bad (*djinn*) spirits. This gives an intriguing historical perspective to the 1976 encounter, suggesting that such entities had been encountered in this location over many centuries.

Such experiences suggest that there is are strong sociological and anthropological aspects to these encounters. Since the early 1970s social scientists have become interested in the cultural implications of such encounters and their approach has been to take UFO research into some radically new areas of enquiry.

Ultraterrestrials

This new approach has become known as the "psychosocial position". It argues that UFOs themselves are not necessarily a physical, "nuts and bolts" phenomena but may be better classified as psychological or sociological events.

This idea has, over the last 40 years or so, divided the UFO research communities. In general terms this is something of a transatlantic issue: North American researchers tend to believe that UFOs are physical objects piloted by extraterrestrials, while European ufologists tend toward the suspicion that the craft may be projections of the human subconscious and that any entities encountered are part of our own psychology. To be clear, this position does not argue that aliens are "hallucinations", more that they manipulate our senses in some way and exist in alternate dimensions of space-time. The accepted term for these beings has become the "ultraterrestrials".

If the UFO-associated aliens are part of the much wider group of ultraterrestrials, what are the mechanisms by which we perceive these beings? Is it a physical process or a spiritual one? I believe that it is both, and that a small, seemingly obscure organ in the centre of the brain may be our communication device.

The mysterious pineal gland

I should like to return to Graham Hancock's observation of the Aboriginal shamanistic belief that the crystalline-like implants placed in the bodies of initiate shamans during the dismemberment process were created during the Dreamtime by "certain very powerful snakes" (see p117). Why snakes? What possible association can be made between a snake and the fabrication of an object? Snakes are unusual in that they have no limbs. If this were simply a legend, then why didn't the Aboriginal ancestors choose an animal that had at least a basic ability to manipulate physical objects – for example, a kangaroo using its forelimbs?

Not only this, but the snake symbolism continues. The shaman has a "snake" placed inside their head. Presumably, by this they mean the centre of the head.

This reminds me of a curious notion recorded by Israeli psychologist Benny Shanon and quoted on the introductory page of his book *The Antipodes of the Mind*. It is a record of a conversation Shanon had with an indigenous shaman (earning his living as, of all things, an ice-cream vendor) in the Peruvian Amazon. The vendor explained:

> God wanted to hide his secrets in a secure place. "Would I put them on the moon?" He reflected. "But then, one day human beings could get there, and it could be that those who would arrive there would not be worthy of the secret knowledge. Or perhaps I should hide them in the depths of the ocean." God entertained this other possibility. But again, for the same reasons, he dismissed it. Then the solution occurred to Him: "I shall put my secrets in the inner sanctum of man's own mind. Then only those who really deserve it will be able to get to it.[10]

As for the snake symbolism, this can also be linked to Gnosticism. One group of Gnostics, known as the Ophites, argued that the Fall of Man described in Genesis had been incorrectly interpreted. For the Ophites, the serpent wanted Adam and Eve, the first man and woman, to eat from the Tree of Knowledge (*gnosis*) so that they would know their true identities and "be like God" (Genesis 3.5). The serpent in this view is interpreted as a messenger of the spiritual god, and the other god, who sought to prevent Adam and Eve from eating the fruit of the Tree of Knowledge, is viewed as the Demiurge. The name Ophites is taken from the ancient Greek word *ophis*, which means "serpent". Of further significance is the snake-like attributes of certain djinn as described in the Islamic texts. We have here a distinct theme across multiple cultures and geographical regions.

So why this preoccupation with snakes being placed in the centre of the head? Well, I know from personal experience that the sensation of small creatures moving around in a location deep behind the eyes is more than just a legend or myth: I know it is real. And I suspect I know what has caused it.

In my 2013 book *The Infinite Mindfield* I describe in detail my powerful session on a device then known simply as Lucia No. 3 and now as the "Hypnagogic Light Experience". For full details on exactly what this is machine is, please turn to the book itself. For now I want to focus on one specific aspect of my experience one afternoon and evening in Switzerland. I make no apology for the extensive quotation that follows – when you have finished reading it, you will realize its relevance to the central theme of this book:

> After "Lucia" was switched off our small group, Dr Winkler, Dr Proeckl, our host [the near-death experience researcher Evelyn Elsaesser-Valarino], and another guest that weekend, Dr Art Funkhouser, discussed the mechanism by which the device can generate such imagery within the brain. As the guys chatted I started to feel a very strange sensation in the centre of my forehead. I didn't comment on it at the time because I didn't wish to deflect attention away

from the subject matter. The sensation felt as if a very small creature was moving just underneath my skin. Indeed, I had a vision in my mind of a baby snake moving inside an egg and about to break out. This sensation continued for about ten minutes and then it subsided. Later that evening over dinner the sensation started again, only this time it had changed to be a slow, precise throbbing. Again, after about ten minutes, it stopped.

I then retired to bed and fell into a very deep sleep. In my dreams I experienced vivid images of snakes coiling around each other. These snakes were brightly coloured and seemed to have intelligence about them. One of them looked straight at me, not into my eyes but at a location just above them. This startled me and I awoke to feel the throbbing sensation in my forehead. I lay in bed intrigued about what was happening. I rationalized that the snake dream had been subliminally stimulated by the snake-like writhings in my forehead. As we know, dream-imagery can be related to bodily sensations, and I assured myself that this was the reason for the dream. However, this did not explain the movement in my head. This was, in some way, related to "Lucia" and its light stimulation.

On my return to the UK the sensation continued, particularly during times of creative writing. It was as if the sensation facilitated the creativity or the creativity facilitated the sensation. I discussed it with friends and associates and the general consensus of opinion was that "Lucia" had opened up my *ajna* or brow *chakra*. Now I have never been interested in such things, which probably explains why I had not made any association between the sensations and this belief. I was further surprised to discover that some mystics have long linked the brow *chakra* with the pineal gland, a small organ nestling in the centre of the brain and located in a direct line from the centre of the forehead. The source of my surprise was that in their articles on the hypnagogic light device Dr Winkler and Dr Proeckl suggest that the light given off by "Lucia" stimulates the pineal gland.[11]

So what exactly is the pineal gland, and why do I suspect that it has a direct relationship with egregorial encounters?

The human brain is the size of a coconut, the shape of a walnut, the colour of uncooked liver and the consistency of firm jelly. It has two hemispheres, which are covered in a thin skin of deeply wrinkled grey tissue called the cerebral cortex. If you slice the brain in two down the centre line, so that the two hemispheres fall apart, you will notice something very odd. You will see that beneath the cortex is a weird jumble of lumps, tubes and chambers. A closer look will tell you that these small structures come in twos: each structure has its twin, or mirror image. These organs are collectively known as the "limbic system". However, on closer inspection you will notice that one of these organs sits in splendid isolation. This tiny reddish-grey object, about the size of a grain of rice, is found in all animals. Because of its odd singularity, it has been an object of profound interest for hundreds, if not thousands, of years. In shape it is reminiscent of a tiny pine cone.

This appearance led to its being called the "pineal" gland. An earlier, and profoundly significant, name is the "epiphysis" (from the Greek, word meaning to "grow" or "bring forth").

The anomalous nature of this organ led ancient cultures to see it as significant. Many thought it to be the "third eye", the place where the soul could look inwards into worlds within, just as the eyes looked outwards at the world outside.

Interestingly, modern scientific advances have shown that this organ not only lives up to its reputation for enigma but also that the ancients made surprisingly accurate observations about its function. For example, our advanced skills in medical dissection have shown that the front section of the pineal gland contains all the structures found in the human eye. It should therefore be unsurprising that research has shown that cold-blooded (poikilothermic) animals perceive light through their pineal gland.[12] This may be significant for human development. It has long been suggested that as the foetus develops within the womb it goes through its own mirror-image of evolution. It is logical to conclude that at some stage it will go through the poikilothermic stage. If this is the case, then this should be when the pineal gland is light-sensitive – and is, in effect, a genuine "third eye".

It is now known that the pineal gland has a crucial role in the generation of the chemical compound melatonin. Known as the "hormone of darkness", this substance is secreted into the blood by the pineal gland as a way of telling the body that it is getting dark and that the organism needs to sleep.

In order to facilitate this, there has to be a mechanism whereby the pineal gland, buried deep within the skull, can differentiate between light and dark. Experiments have shown that the photoreceptors in the retina send a signal along the retinohypothalmic tract to the suprachiasmatic nucleus (SCN), and a similar signal follows a route along the upper thoracic spinal column to the superior cervical ganglion whose post-ganglionic sympathetic fibres innervate the pineal gland. On receipt of this signal an enzyme, serotonin-N-acetyltransferase (NAT), is released within the pineal gland; and this, in turn, generates the production of melatonin.

However, there is evidence that the light sensitivity of the pineal gland is designed to detect light from a source other than the retina. Vestigial photo-receptivity within the pineal gland has been suggested by the discovery of pigmented cells arranged in a rosette-like structure reminiscent of developing retinal structures. This discovery suggests that the human pineal gland exhibits transient cellular features reminiscent of developing photoreceptor cells as found in other mammals. In effect, the pineal gland is similar to an eye. Furthermore, in

1970 the light-sensitive compound phosphorus was discovered within the pineal gland.

Thirty-seven years later, in 2007, an intriguing experiment took place at the National University in Taiwan – one that suggested that maybe it is a different, less literal form of light that the pineal gland is designed to process, the light that is found in the often-misunderstood word "enlightenment".

A small team led by Lyh-Horng Chen studied 20 subjects, 11 men and 9 women, who practised the Chinese meditation technique known as "Chinese original quiet sitting".

The subjects volunteered to have their brains scanned using the medical process of fMRI (functional magnetic resonance imaging). This measures changes in blood flow within the brain and, in doing so, can show which parts of the brain are active when the subject is thinking about particular tasks or concepts. In other words, it can measure "thought".

All the subjects were then asked to recite some of the traditional mantras that are used as part of this spiritual technique. By repeating these phrases, the adherents are led to fall into deep meditative states similar to those experienced by the Tibetan Bön. Interestingly, each subject showed increased activity in the pineal gland during these exercises. In a report in the UK magazine *New Scientist*, Chen concluded:

There is no definition of "soul" in the scientific field. However, our results demonstrate a correlation between pineal activation and religious meditation which might have profound implications in the physiological understanding of mind, spirit and soul.[13]

Here we have evidence that the pineal gland is significant for something more than conventional physiology. However, such results, telling us that something is happening within the pineal gland, do not tell us what is happening at these times, and where the information is sourced to create these internal journeys to other states of awareness.

If the pineal gland is some kind of portal between the Kenoma and the Pleroma, then we need to investigate the practicalities of such a claim. How do ordinary people open up this portal and what tools can be used to access the egregorial world? This will be our task for the third part of this book.

PART THREE

ACCESSING THE EGREGORIAL REALM

CHAPTER 10
THE NATURAL LIMINALS

I should now like us to turn our attention to circumstances whereby awareness of the liminal area between the Kenoma and the Pleroma can be accessed under natural circumstances – that is to say, without the aid of mind-altering substances such as psychedelics or entheogens (we will look at this subject in the next chapter).

Much earlier in our discussions we encountered the strange dream of Enoch as described in the Gnostic text *The Book of the Secrets of Enoch*. Here, Enoch describes how two men appeared in his bedroom and took him into the sky to show him the "Seven Heavens". Significantly, he is already in a dream state when he first encounters the Egregorials. He writes:

> And I lay on my bed sleeping. And, while I slept, a great distress entered my heart, and I was weeping with my eyes in a dream. And I could not figure out what this distress might be, [nor] what might be happening to me. Then two huge men appeared to me, the like of which I had never seen on earth. […] And they stood at the head of my bed and called me by my name. Then I awoke from my sleep, and saw those men, standing in front of me, in actuality.[1]

Enoch's account has elements of a phenomenon now known as "sleep paralysis". Although he does not actually describe the feeling of constriction in the chest and the disturbing feeling of paralysis, it is clear that what he experienced was a related phenomenon. Take, for example, the appearance of unearthly entities in the room. Here we have an overlap from a dream state into reality, as Enoch, believing he has woken up, finds that the dream entities are still there. It is as if these entities have used Enoch's dream state to come through from the Pleroma to the Kenoma.

In its purer form, sleep paralysis involves the victim waking up in the middle of the night and finding they are being pinned down on the bed by something massive sitting on their chest. This sensation is a feeling of complete helplessness and body-wide paralysis. Recorded throughout history, this is not at all a rare phenomenon. Recent surveys among a variety of populations around the world suggest that between 20 to 40 per cent of people experience at least one incidence of sleep paralysis in their lifetimes.

It therefore comes as no surprise to discover that virtually all languages have a word for the experience. Of particular significance is the German term *Alpdruck*, which literally means "elf pressure". In Thailand it is known as *phi um*, or "ghost covered", and in Japan as *kanashibari*, or "bound by metal". Another intriguing and pertinent term is the Egyptian Arabic *kabus*, which is our source for the word "incubus".

Of course, modern neurology and psychology have an explanation for these experiences. The process by which a dream overlaps into what seems like sensory reality is known as "REM [rapid eye movement] intrusion". This is where the person is actually asleep and dreaming but a part of the brain is still awake and processing the sights and sounds of the external world. Any dream images are then projected into the external world and seem to be part of it. In this way, a dream can seem to be "real".

When we sleep, the body protects itself from dream-induced bodily damage by stopping the dreamer from acting out any physical actions they may wish to perform in the dream state – for example, hitting out at a dream attacker. If they were to mirror this hitting out by moving their arms, they might hurt themselves – or somebody in the bed with them. By paralysing the body in this way, the brain protects us. However, if one happens to become semi-conscious in such a state, the sensation of paralysis can be terrifying, particularly if accompanied by a feeling that an alien entity is responsible.

It is for this reason that sleep paralysis is also known as a "night-mare". The word *mare* comes from the same root as the German *Mahr* and the Old Norse *mara*, referring to a supernatural being that lies on peoples' chests at night. It is thought that the original source of the word *mare* is the Indo-European word *mar* which means to pound, bruise or crush. If this is the case, then this is evidence that sleep paralysis has been experienced for thousands of years and has always been part of our perceptual universe.

Particularly relevant to our enquiry is that a regular perception accompanying sleep paralysis is of beeping or humming noises. Here is an example cited by anthropologist Shelley Adler:

> My experience was accompanied by a vibration or electric sound in my head that is like a humming or static. I am not sure if it is a noise or a feeling, maybe both.[2]

As well as the entity sitting on the chest or pinning the person down on the bed, another being is also sometimes sensed. Known in various traditions as the "old hag", this is usually seen as a cowled figure in a corner of the room or standing at the end of the bed. In times past, the being holding the person down would have been identified as an incubus or succubus: male and female vampire-like beings. Modern-day encounters, such as that described by my mother with her "grey", may involve aliens as well as ghosts. What is clear here is that these experiences are absolutely terrifying. Could the motivation here be the generation of fear? Paul Eno would argue that sleep paralysis is far more than simply a neurological effect, and that such encounters are in some way created by the Parasites in order to gain sustenance (see p140).

Closely related to sleep paralysis are the experiences of hypnagogia and hypnopompia. The former takes place as a person is going to sleep and the latter as they are waking up. These again are circumstances whereby dream imagery can be perceived in semi-awareness. The dream imagery can sometimes overlay external reality and, in doing so, can seemingly transport the person to other locations or, in other circumstances, can bring about encounters with other intelligences. Of course, we have a choice of whether we consider such dream intrusions as simply hallucinations or else interpret them as glimpses of another reality that abuts onto our own.

Whatever our interpretations of these liminal states of consciousness, they are naturally created. They happen spontaneously and seem to be a common element of the human condition.

In this chapter we will review various aspects of these natural experiences and discover what they can tell us about egregorial encounters.

Childhood

That children seem to have special abilities that allow them to perceive Egregorials has long been recognized in occult and magical circles. For example, in his introduction to *The Book of the Sacred Magic of Abramelin the Mage*, occultist Samuel McGregor Mathers makes the following observation:

> The idea of the employment of a Child as Clairvoyant in the invocation of the Guardian Angel is not unusual; for example, in the "Mendal", a style of Oriental Divination familiar to all readers of Wilkie Collins' novel, *The Moonstone*, ink is poured into the palm of a Child's hand, who, after certain mystical words being recited by the Operator, beholds visions clairvoyantly therein.

The celebrated evocation at which the great Medieval sculptor, Benvenuto Cellini, is said to have assisted, also was in part worked by the aid of a Child as Seer.[3]

Interestingly, the Greeks believed that pre-pubescent children were perfect mediums for direct communication with the egregorial world. They can certainly be adept in, for example, scrying. Indeed, children, or child-like beings, have sometimes been seen as entities during scrying sessions. On a number of occasions the Egregorials who came through during the scrying sessions of John Dee and Edward Kelley were children (see p70). And this theme carries right through to the 21st century.

You will recall that in my coverage of the creation of the tulpa known as Philip Aylesford by Iris Owen and her associates at the Toronto Society for Psychical Research, we discussed how psychologist Dr Joel Whitton suggested that the creation of Philip may have been facilitated by the group entering a collective manifestation of a child ego-state and in doing so opening a much sublimated right-brain group-spirit (see p96).

In 2007 British author Michael J Hallowell published a book entitled *Invizikids: The Curious Enigma of "Imaginary" Childhood Friends*. In this he presented a fascinating analysis of how young children often describe having friends that nobody else can see. Hallowell calls these entities "Invizikids". He acknowledges the standard psychological explanation that children lacking brothers and sisters invent these pretend friends because they are lonely. However, the phenomenon is regularly recorded in children who have siblings. In this case, the commonplace explanation is that this is an attempt at uniqueness and having friends of one's own that have no relationship with one's siblings. As Hallowell points out, these two "explanations" are totally contradictory: imaginary friends are invented either because a child has no siblings or because he or she does have them.

Hallowell took the time to interview over 100 people from across the world, all of whom had had encounters with imaginary friends. He uses the term non-corporeal companions (NCCs) to describe these entities. He notes certain constants, one of which is intriguing to anyone who agrees with Paul Eno's model of the Parasites – namely, that although the entities never physically hurt their companions, they regularly, and sometimes perversely, frighten them. Eno has argued that it is fear the Parasites feed on. Another constant is that in most cases the visitations begin at around age three and end at the onset of puberty. We shall return later to the question of why this may be. Finally, the entities, when asked directly about their origins, are always extremely vague. This suggests that they are not what they appear or, indeed, claim to be. The stock answers with regard to origins are "from far away" or "from another place". Another particularly relevant and not uncommon answer is that they live on a vehicle which is always on the move.

Hallowell has placed his NCCs into four categories; the Invizikids, the Elementals, the Animals and the Wackies.

Most common are the Invizikids. As their name suggests, they are only ever seen by the child in question. These entities act as any normal child would do: they sneeze, cough and are even described as eating food. Curiously, 30 per cent of cases have involved these beings identifying themselves as having double-word names – I have personal experience of this in that my sister Sandra had from the age of three until around six an NCC called "Me-Me". Hallowell found this curious affectation all across the world. For example, he found a Gardu-Gardu in the Philippines, a Manno-Manno in Bangladesh and a Bally-Bally in South Yorkshire, UK.

Invizikids use invisibility on a regular basis. Sometimes they disappear when another child or adult enters the room, which suggests they might have been seen otherwise. More usually, they remain invisible to the other person while remaining visible to their special friend.

My own reading around this subject suggests that this invisibility is not a constant. I was particularly struck by a section in psychologist Dr Serena Roney-Dougal's fascinating book *The Faery Faith* where the author tells of a friend of hers whose daughter had an imaginary friend. Late one evening this adult friend decided to take a photograph of her daughter while the child was asleep. When the photograph was developed, the image clearly showed another child asleep in the bed with the girl. On being shown the photograph, the child immediately identified the other little girl as her imaginary friend.[4]

What can we make of this? To create an image on film, an object has to reflect light and in doing so should be visible to the naked eye; and yet the mother saw nothing unusual when she took the photograph. This suggests that the NCC had some unusual form of three-dimensional reality that was picked up by a camera but not by the eye.

In connection with our own enquiries, Hallowell's second category is of particular interest. His "Elementals" almost always live outdoors, often in remote areas or by the coast. Significantly, children regularly describe these entities as "pixies" or "little goblins" or something similar. These entities are not particularly friendly: they seem to be emotionally detached, more observers of the child than good friends. We again have this sense of liminality, the idea that these intelligences find it easier to come through in certain peripheral locations, such as the Celtic fringe of the British Isles. It would be interesting to know how many of these Elemental NCC encounters took place in Wales, Cornwall, the Highlands of Scotland and the West of Ireland. Another key point with regard to Elemental NCCs is that they regularly appear in numbers, rather than the single-friend scenario of the more house-bound Invizikids. This suggests to me that they are not the same phenomenon.

We now move to the most disturbing category of NCCs; the Animals. These can be dogs, cats, rabbits or birds. As we have already discovered, many precursors to UFO abduction cases involve encounters with rabbits, hares and, most suggestively, owls. This variation of the NCC phenomenon is reported both inside and outside. The entities look like normal animals but with two typically egregorial skills: they can appear and disappear at will; and they can speak. In the latter regard, Hallowell makes an important observation. His research suggests that, in contrast to the other categories of NCCs, the voices of this variety have been heard by others. This suggests an objective reality outside the imagination of the companion.

The final category, called the "Wackies" by Hallowell, are also intriguing. He breaks these down into two subtypes: Sages and Animates. The Sages are teachers and usually manifest as a member of a culturally or ethnically different type from the companion. For example, they may appear as a Native American medicine man, a Chinese Mandarin or an Inuit shaman. Also regularly reported are the cowled figures we know so well from cases of sleep paralysis.

I would argue that Wackies are of a totally different type to the other three NCCs. They present powerful shamanistic themes and suggest that the companion is involved in some kind of shamanic journey. Sages always appear as adults and impart guidance and wisdom to the child. I would like to suggest that this may be related more to my Daemon-Eidolon Dyad than my egregorial model: for further information on this please consult my books *The Daemon: A Guide to Your Extraordinary Secret Self* and *Opening the Doors of Perception*.

Animates (inanimate objects taking on sentience and conversing with the companion) are also intriguing, suggesting an experience similar to that created by psychedelics such as LSD and DMT.

The big general question behind NCCs is why is it that young children, and adults who can reproduce a child-like ego state, perceive such entities? Is it simply an active imagination at work, or something more?

I suspect it may be related to brain development. The brain consists of approximately 100 billion neurons. These are cells that receive and transmit electrochemical signals via other neurons. Neurons are long, thin cells that look a little like trees with branches going in all directions, sometimes for many inches.

Through this network each individual neuron is connected to around 10,000 other neurons. Modern science believes that somewhere within this vast web of signals and junctions your own self, with all your hopes and dreams, is located.

Imagine that each neuron is like an electrical cable used to transfer an electric current from one location to another – for example, a cable that runs from an amplifier to a speaker in a hi fi system. In the core of the cable is a copper wire, and it is this that carries the electrical signal. To stop the electricity leaking out, the wire is insulated using another kind of material that is electrically non-conductive. This is wrapped round the wire throughout its length. The insulating material in neurons is called myelin. This is a white fatty substance consisting of a countless number of cells called oligodendrocytes that wrap their branch-like extensions around the neuron.

It is known that the removal of myelin disrupts communication across the brain. In effect, each neuron can become isolated from every other neuron because their electrochemical signals literally leak out into the surrounding brain tissue.

However, at birth much of the brain is not myelinated. Information just leaks out. This means that the communication speed of signals across the brain of a newly born infant is 16 times less efficient than that of an adult. As the baby ages, the number of fully myelinated neurons increases. By the time the child is around 15 years old, the brain is fully insulated.

Could all this in some way be responsible for a child's perception of egregorial entities such as Hallowell's NCCs? Note that repeatedly in this book we have been presented with examples of how such entities impose themselves into the perceptual world of youngsters. This stops for many at puberty and slightly later, coinciding with the complete insulation of the brain.

The word "insulate" literally means to make something into an island, to isolate it from a wider world. Does the process of myelination "insulate" the adult brain from a wider reality? Does myelin effectively close our "doors of perception"?

If so, how may this work? At the end of my book *Opening the Doors of Perception* I discuss recent discoveries regarding the role of glial cells within the brain. These outnumber the neurons at a ratio of ten to one. Indeed, this is where the popular and much misunderstood phrase "we only use ten per cent of our brain" comes from. I would like to suggest that the electrochemical communications in pre-pubescent children leak out into the glial cells and the glial cells take over their cross-brain communications.

Unlike neurons, glial cells do not conduct electrochemical signals. Indeed, until recently their purpose was a complete mystery. The word "glial" comes from the German for "glue", and this is what, for many years, it was believed their purpose was. But in 1989 a team of researchers at Yale University Medical School discovered that glial cells have their own form of communication and that this is much more efficient than that used by the neurons. It is facilitated by something known as an "intercellular calcium wave". Like a wave, this spreads out from its source in all directions, rather than the single direction facilitated by neurons.[5]

In his book *The Root of Thought* neuroscientist Andrew Koob argues that glial cells and calcium waves are directly responsible for thought.[6] Koob is fascinated by the generation of imagery in dreams and during periods of sensory deprivation. In an interview published in *Scientific American* in October 2009 he made this astounding claim regarding astrocytes, by far the most abundant glial cells associated with neuronal synapses:

Without input from our senses through neurons, how is it that we have such vivid thoughts? How is it that when we are deep in thought we seemingly shut off everything in the environment around us? In this theory, neurons are tied to our muscular action and external senses. We know astrocytes monitor neurons for this information. Similarly, they can induce neurons to fire. Therefore, astrocytes modulate neuron behavior. This could mean that calcium waves in astrocytes are our thinking mind.[7]

Is it the dependence upon the glial network as the neurons slowly myelinate themselves that allows youngsters to perceive elements of the Pleroma?

I cannot help making the analogy between an analogue telephone system and the non-local information transfer facilitated by the Internet. Could it be that we adults are restricted by the poor bandwidth that our electrochemical neuronal process gives us, whereas children are happily surfing the Pleromic Internet?

Earlier we discussed the dual mysteries of "consciousness" and "reality". We discovered that what we believe to be a consistent, solid, material universe presented to us by our senses has none of these qualities. We have also found that the perceiver of these sensory impressions is likewise immaterial in its true nature, in that self-aware consciousness itself cannot be physically located in space.

What we really have, in the simplest terms, is nothing experiencing nothing by means of nothing. We have also discussed the belief that there is a hidden reality behind this one, known as the Pleroma, a place that contains what the ancient Greek philosopher Plato called the Forms. These are the archetypes whose facsimiles can be found within the Kenoma, the everyday world.

In *The Republic*, written around 380 BCE, Plato presented an analogy to explain how perception of these two realities (the Pleroma and the Kenoma) may function.

In the relevant passage Plato has his mentor Socrates describe the condition of a group of prisoners who had spent their whole lives staring at the back wall of a cave. They are all chained in such a way that they can only ever direct their eyes toward the cave wall. Behind them is a large fire which is kept alight at all times. Midway between the prisoners and the fire is an elevated walkway. Here people occasionally walk along, carrying with them cut-outs and puppets "of men and other living things". These shapes are projected as shadows on the cave wall. This is the only visual perceptions the prisoners have. The shadows are, for them, the totality of what is real. The prisoners, all sharing this same perceptual reality, give names to the various shadows they see.

One day, one of the prisoners manages to loosen his chains and free himself. He turns around, sees the fire, and beyond it the cave entrance. Walking through the entrance he sees, for the first time, true reality illuminated by the sun. He sees the light beyond the light, the light that had been obscured by the flames of the fire. Excitedly he returns to tell the other prisoners. Still trapped, looking at the shadows on the wall, his associates tell him that he is crazy: all that really exists, they say, are the shadows.[8]

Plato, through his character Socrates, uses the cave analogy to show that what we believe to be reality is simply a reflection of another, genuinely real world that exists beyond our normal senses. This higher perceptual world, which I call the Pleroma, is denied to most of us, as the British poet William Blake wrote, in an attempt to explain his own experiences with egregorial entities and making direct reference to Plato's cave, in his book *The Marriage of Heaven and Hell:*

If the doors of perception were cleansed every thing would appear to man as it is, Infinite. For man has closed himself up, till he sees all things thro' narrow chinks of his cavern.[9]

The mysterious owls

To round off this section on Michael J Hallowell's non-corporeal companions, and before we move on to another area that gives support to my model of Egregorials, I would like to focus in on one area of children's perceptions of the Pleroma: the significance of owls or, more accurately, Egregorials taking on the image of owls. We have already noted how these birds feature in many Paleolithic cave paintings.

The association between these enigmatic nocturnal birds and shamanic experiences has carried through the centuries. You will recall how, in 1890, the 30-year-old Gitksan (Tsimshian) shaman Isaac Tens began his own shamanic initiation after a series of encounters with owl-like entities (see p20).

This imagery has continued into the 20th century and has now become associated with alien abduction. Whitley Strieber's initial abduction encounter, for instance, started with a series of hypnagogic owl images, followed by the sight of a large barn owl staring at him through the window of his log cabin.

Here is a fascinating case from 1926 which involves "owl imagery" many years before the UFO-abduction scenario became part of popular culture. The experience involved a young boy who had been playing hide-and-seek around the area of his home in north London. He decided to hide behind an open gate he found at the back of a house. He looked through the window of the house to see three figures dressed in silvery grey suits, seemingly made of tubes of rubber, like thinner versions of the Michelin Man. The central figure turned around and saw him through the window. He later described this being as resembling a large owl with a "wide black eyepiece".

In his classic review of abductions, *Passport to the Cosmos*, Harvard Medical School psychiatrist John E Mack describes how many of his subjects, particularly those whose abduction scenarios took place in childhood, described owl encounters during their experiences. For example, "Carol" described to Mack how, on her first encounter with alien entities, a huge owl came down to her from out of the sky then hovered close to her face. She said that its "big dark eyes" took up "three quarters" of its head.[10]

Carol's continuing encounters took place in vivid dream states. One of these particularly intrigued me. She describes how the dream began with a "high-pitched buzzing sound". She finds herself lying on her back on a hillside. She is unable to move. Then she spots an object in the sky spiralling down toward her.

Next, she is surrounded by a bright light and the descending object comes closer and appears to be an owl. She is able to turn her head away from looking upwards to see, standing next to her, a shaman-like figure wearing a heavy fur coat and an antler head dress. She identifies this being as Cernunnos, the half-animal, half-human Celtic deity. It is then that the owl comes closer to her, looking directly at her with its huge black eyes. She feels a heavy weight on her chest and body before waking up.[11]

As we have seen, buzzing sounds, together with powerful bodily vibrations, are associated with out-of-body experiences, as well as many classic UFO encounters. This connection is reinforced by her description of not being able to move: this is classic sleep paralysis. You will recall that in my mother's encounter with the "grey", she described how she could not move as she watched the fingers come around the edge of the door (p2).

In an earlier book, *Abductions*, John E Mack describes the childhood alien encounters of a subject he calls Colin.[12] When Colin was two and a half, he frequently complained to his parents that he had been "taken by scary owls" which had "floated down" from the sky. This is a close echo of the description given by Carol of her owl dream.

If we now return to the 1926 case involving the young boy and the three Egregorials, it is notable that his owl-like creature was accompanied by two beings uncannily similar to modern-day greys. The boy described how they had pale "light bulb"-shaped heads and dark, slit-like eyes, no obvious nose and slit-like mouths.

In all three of the above cases, covering more than half a century, we have significant parallels with my mother's encounter in 2012. Carol's owl's "huge black eyes" mirrors the eyes of the entity that appeared in my mother's bedroom, while in the 1926 case it is the slit-like mouth that catches the young boy's attention – again uncannily reminiscent of my mother's description. When we link these three cases with the entities depicted in the 10,000-year-old cave paintings at Hoshangabad (p12) and the strange statues found at Ayn Ghazal (p23), we see a pattern developing.

Furthermore, on coming across this case, I was immediately struck by how Carol's dream imagery seemed to have ingredients of various ancient cave paintings, specifically an image known as the Sorcerer in the Trois Frères caves, in Ariège, southwest France. Graham Hancock makes a similar association in his book *Supernatural: Meetings with the Ancient Teachers of Mankind*.[13]

Thus, it seems there is a clear link between egregorial encounters in childhood and old age. I would now like explore this possibly significant association. Firstly, we will look at encounters of the very young, then turn our attention to the very old.

Shamanic-like childhood encounters

In his book *The Omega Project*, near-death experience researcher Dr Kenneth Ring argues, as I do, that altered states of consciousness can tell us a great deal about the true nature of reality. He cites many reports of non-human encounters. Some of these struck me as being highly shamanic in their structure. For example, in one of Ring's cases the subject describes how, as a child, they sensed, in an altered state of consciousness, that they were falling into a hole in the ground, rather than being raised up in the air as many UFO-related abductions seem to require. Descending into a world below us is a standard shamanic motif and also has elements of the themes explored by Lewis Carroll in *Alice in Wonderland*. Here is the account in question:

> At age six, while in bed for the night in my own room, I saw a strange-looking "man" at my window. It was a second-floor room, but there was a landing outside that window. I was scared as the "man" didn't look right. He was small, about my height, with a big funny head, and with no hair and scary, big black eyes. He knew my name, he called me out. I suddenly wasn't afraid anymore. I got out of bed and went out the window with him. I just kind of went through it.[14]

It could be argued that such dream imagery is related to the cultural power of alien representations in movies such as *Close Encounters of the Third Kind* and *ET*. But the creature does not resemble these cinematic aliens.

Ring is famous for his writings on the near-death experience, and I find it fascinating that he has shifted his attention to alien encounters, specifically those experienced by children. One case that particularly caught my attention is that of Lori Demera. She was five years old at the time. This is how a much older Lori described what happened to her:

> I remember standing in the middle of the huge spiral my dad had mowed in a field for me. I was looking up. A bright metal craft came straight down. Next thing I remember is a small white creature (man?) talking to me. He had huge black eyes and was bald. He talked to me about my destiny which was related to cleaning up [the] earth's environment. Then I was walking back to my home.[15]

Here we have a classic "grey". It is unclear what year this event took place, but it is fair to assume it was many years before such imagery appeared in the public consciousness, and even if it had, we are discussing here the experience of a five-year-old child, not a teenager or adult for whom such imagery would be available via books or movies.

The next incident took place in 1959. It again involves a being uncannily similar to a grey. It is important to stress that in the 1950s and into the early 1960s the general reports of UFO entities involved beings similar to the classic "bug-eyed monsters" or else the "Nordics", tall, blonde and generally human-like "space brothers" here to save humanity from nuclear destruction. Yet again a girl (this time a nine-year-old) has a terrifying encounter while wandering in a German forest. The episode has elements of Faery encounters:

> I began to have a sense of being watched. I suddenly found myself face to face with a strange being. He was about my height, luminous and wearing what appeared to be a luminous reflective suit without seams. He had a triangular face with large cat-like eyes. I had the sense that he was surprised I could see him or had found him.[16]

This encounter seemed to stimulate in the subject a spontaneous ability to enter what she was later to term "altered states of consciousness". She felt she was on the edge of a "different reality".

Her younger brother, who had been three at the time of the incident, confirmed what she had seen when the family revisited the forest in Germany and the topic came up in general conversation. She mentioned that something weird had happened to her. His response was to ask if it had involved the "monkey-like" creature. Lisa was stunned by this revelation. Here was proof that what she had seen had been shared by her brother. Her comment about the trip had stimulated a repressed memory in her brother. It is interesting to speculate whether any adult present would also have seen the creature.

Some children's "alien" encounters suggest that the already discussed Charles Bonnet Syndrome may be involved. For example, consider this case reported in *Fortean Times* magazine in a readers' contribution section called "It Happened to Me". Correspondent Paula Simms describes an incident in her childhood that evidences links between NCCs and UFO encounters. She describes how, when she was nearly seven years of age, in the summer of 1954, she was suffering from hay fever and was confined to her bedroom. Her school friends sometimes visited, and one day, as a joke, she told them a story about dragons living under her bed. Her friends, in response to the story, looked under the bed and responded with shock. Wondering what was going on, Paula looked to see what had startled them:

> So I bent down expecting to see nothing and was amazed to see two smallish green-faced beings in what were later to be called space suits with large globes around their heads. They were carrying large see-through gun-like things with three different coloured rays showing and when I looked at them they seemed as shocked to see me as I was to see them.[17]

Intriguingly, this was not a lonely child creating an hallucination but an experience shared by other children. Furthermore, the alien imagery is also significant. Although, as Paula rightly says, the space suit was something from the future and the early 1960s, it is fair to say that such images were popular in science fiction magazines of the time. However, as I mentioned before, it is unlikely that a six-year-old would have been aware of such images.

In addition, of course, the similarities to Charles Bonnet hallucinations cannot be ignored. However, most reports of

Charles Bonnet Syndrome involve elderly individuals, not young children. This suggests to me that Charles Bonnet-like experiences can take place at any age. Simply by entering an altered state of consciousness, it seems that anybody can experience glimpses of the Pleroma. All that is needed is a process whereby such states can be accessed automatically. This was something that intrigued American neuroscientist Dr John Cunningham Lilly.

John Lilly and inner space

John Cunningham Lilly (1915–2001), having become fascinated by the UFO abduction phenomenon, was keen to understand the psychological and neurological nature of the experience. This ambition had been nurtured by his fascination with the writings of Irish philosopher George Berkeley, specifically Berkeley's model of subjective idealism – the same model of reality that stimulated Dr Samuel Johnson's stone-kicking episode, as mentioned earlier (p4).

Lilly became a pioneer of research into altered states of consciousness. He believed that periods of sensory deprivation could facilitate such states, having noted that many UFO-related encounters took place when the witness was in a state of low sensory stimulation, such as driving along on a long straight country road late at night or else in a quasi-sleep state. In his view, in experiencing such conditions a person may seamlessly move into what is known as a "waking lucid dream state". (This is when a person remains, or becomes, self-aware whilst experiencing a dream. Under these circumstances the dream state becomes superimposed over the waking perceptual world.)

In 1953 he developed the first experimental use of an isolation tank whilst working for the US Public Health Service Commissioned Officers Corps. This technique became known as REST (Restricted Environmental Stimulation Technique).

In 1973 he published his book *The Centre of the Cyclone: An Autobiography of Inner Space*. Here he describes his own experiences in states of sensory deprivation. One of them was particular relevant to this enquiry. He found himself in a large, open space bathed in a light that had no obvious source. He knew there were two entities with him. These were filling his mind with information, such a great amount of data that he felt he was approaching overload. At this point the entities told him that he could either stay in this location or else return back to Earth. If he did decide to leave, he was told that they would give him an assignment to fulfil at some time in the future. They said he would forget this when he returned to Earth, but they would bring the information to his waking mind when they needed him. He decided to return.

From his own experiences, Lilly concluded that there were nine levels of consciousness. In addition to our familiar waking consciousness within consensual reality, (0) there are four negative levels below this one and four positive levels above. Within the "normal" level a human being effectively functions as a robot: all that is needed for effective survival is programmed responses to external stimuli. Indeed, for much of our lives this is what we do. We observe the external world and react to it.

Consciousness in each of the positive levels become increasingly less mechanical. Most of us have perceived Level One above consensual space. This is when a person becomes really interested in something – for example, when researching a topic or being lost in the moment. He or she becomes absorbed in whatever has their attention. Level Two is what we call "bliss". This is a feeling of belonging to a wider, living world. French dramatist Roman Rolland called this the Oceanic Feeling. The mind expands outside the confines of the everyday self and senses that it is part of something greater. This can sometimes be achieved by the non-intellectual reaction we have when we listen to a great piece of music or are touched by powerful poetry. For Lilly it is at Level Three that we can commune with other entities, such as the two he encountered in his sensory deprivation state. He argues that in this state we can also become telepathic and find ourselves having an out-of-body experience. There is a fourth level but few ever reach this while living. This is Samadhi: union with God.

The four negative levels have various stages of psychic discomfort, from the vague feeling of insecurity when one is criticized, feels nauseous or is hurt in love, through depression, dread or deep-felt fear, to total loneliness and the development of suicidal tendencies. This climaxes with the sensation of fusing with negative entities, with no chance of escape.

Although Lilly was more than happy to experiment with naturally facilitated altered states of consciousness, he was very well aware that a shortcut could be taken by ingesting artificially created substances such as LSD, especially if administered just before a session of sensory deprivation.

In the early 1970s Lilly was conducting a series of seminars at the Esalen Institute in northern California when he was struck down by a powerful migraine headache. His associate, Dr Craig Enright, suggested Lilly might gain some relief by receiving an injection of a drug called ketamine and entering the isolation tank. He found this experience amazing, opening up hitherto undiscovered areas of his subconscious. A week later, Enright and Lilly met again at the Esalen isolation tank. This time they agreed to conduct joint research into the effects of ketamine. What subsequently occurred became dramatized in the 1980 Ken Russell movie *Altered States*. The discoveries made by this pair have an important bearing on the central theme of our enquiry.

In *The Center of the Cyclone* Lilly describes their three conclusions:

First, one's internal reality could differ radically from the external reality in which one was participating, even with regard to prominent features of the physical environment.

Second, the person might remain active physically in the external environment, in a manner not responding closely to one's internal experience of this activity. And third, one could remain totally oblivious to this disparity.[18]

Lilly argued that our perception of external reality is subjective and moulded by our own worldview. This is the point I made earlier with regard to Pierce's concept of the Phaneron. We all exist in our own versions of reality, and that reality is populated by creations of our mind, or Egregorials. Moreover, it must be added, it is these entities that use our consciousness to manifest themselves within the Kenoma.

This is a hugely controversial assertion, I know. What I must now do is present more evidence that the mind can be manipulated to create what is "out there".

Shamanism revisited

We have already looked at the contribution the late Professor John E Mack made with regard to non-human encounters, focusing on his work with young children (p147). But this was not the only area of his enquiry. In his book *Passport to the Cosmos: Human Transformation and Alien Encounters*, Mack discusses the experiences of shaman Bernardo Peixoto, a member of the Uru-e-Wau-Wau tribe of Para state in northern Brazil.

Uru-e-Wau-Wau literally means "people from the stars" in the local language. Legend has it that a *huskerah*, "something descending from the sky", landed in the Amazon basin. From this came a group of small glowing beings with large eyes called the *makuras*, which taught the Uru-e-Wau-Wau how to plant seed and grow corn. Images of these entities, also known as *atojars* (literally "people with so much knowledge they cannot be from Earth"), are incised on cave walls.

This is the cultural environment Bernardo Peixoto grew up in. His father was white Portuguese, his mother a

Uru-e-Wau-Wau. He was ideally positioned, with links to both communities, to become a spokesperson for his people. He was trained as a shaman and also as an academic, receiving his PhD in anthropology from Belém de Para University. His tribal name, one he used interchangeably with his Portuguese name, is Ipupiara Makunaiman.

Bernardo informed Mack that during his training as a shaman, the tribal elders informed him that in the jungle could be found little people identified as the *curipiras*, transdimensional entities residing in the spirit realm but regularly able to become physical, so they could be seen by humans. One specific variation of the *curipiras*, known as the *ikuyas*, take a specific humanoid form uncannily similar to the "greys" of ufology.

These beings are associated with caves and the underworld. For example, Bernardo informed Mack that there was a place near the junction of the Rio Negro and the Amazon river where balls of light had been seen emerging from a hole in the ground.

In his own shamanic travelling Peixoto described to Mack how he had had a series of powerful encounters with entities he described like this:

> Grayish in color, with triangular-shaped faces and pointed chins, like a "dragon-lizard". They had "big, big, big eyes" that were black and slanted.[19]

Yet again, I refer you back to my mother's description of the entity she encountered in her sleep paralysis state. She described a being with huge black eyes and a noticeably pointed chin. How could an elderly lady in the north of England, with no knowledge of flying saucers or the legends of the Amazon basin, describe *exactly* the same entity as a Uru-e-Wau-Wau shaman-anthropologist?

How do isolated communities in the northeast of Brazil come up with exactly the same scenario of entities dwelling underground as the peoples of the Arabian Peninsula?

Why is it that Amerindians feel motivated to create cave paintings showing non-human entities uncannily similar to those depicted on cave paintings in northern India, the Red Centre of Australia and the mountains of South Africa?

All these are questions that demand answers, since the excuse of coincidence is simply inadequate. We are dealing here with encounters across the world and across centuries of time.

There is one final link that may give us an important clue. One of the typical encounters with *ikuyas* described by John E Mack particularly caught my attention:

> Shamans have reported talking with entities that come from the sky, and strange women are said to have taken people to places to show them where special herbs grow.[20]

One of the great puzzles of modern anthropology regarding the tribes of the Upper Amazon relates to the particular hallucinogenic brew, ayahuasca. This is made by combining two ingredients: the bark of a vine named *Banisteriopsis caapi* and the leaves of a plant called *Psychotria viridis*. These are mixed together in a pot of boiling water and left for hours to drain down to a brown liquid. This is then drunk, and complex hallucinations soon ensue. The puzzle is a simple one. As I wrote in my book *The Infinite Mindfield*:

> *Psychotria viridis* contains a powerful psychotropic substance called dimethyltryptamine (DMT). (As we shall discover later, this substance is derived from tryptophan and is structurally analogous with serotonin, melatonin and other psychedelic tryptamines.) DMT is what brings about the hallucinations reported by individuals who ingest ayahuasca. However, if *Psychotria viridis* is taken orally, either in a liquid form or by chewing the leaves, nothing unusual is perceived. This is because of DMT's identical chemical structure to serotonin. As soon as the DMT reaches the gut it will

be rendered inactive by Monoamine oxidase (MAO-A). You can eat and drink as much *Psychotria viridis* as you like but nothing will happen other than you feeling somewhat full and bloated. So how is it that ayahuasca is so effective as a hallucinogen?[21]

The answer is, on the surface, quite simple. It is now known that *Banisteriopsis caapi*, uniquely of the 80,000 known Amazonian plant species, contains three substances that stop the MAO-A from being effective in the gut and, in doing so, enables the hallucinogenic DMT to enter the bloodstream. Once there, DMT is free to cross the blood–brain barrier to activate receptor sites in the brain.

The question then becomes, how did the shamans know which two plants to mix together to make such an effective hallucinogenic drink? It seems that when the anthropologists asked that question of the shamans, they gave a very simple answer: the plants told them. Are these "guides", the "plant spirits", encountered during shamanic travelling, just another variation of the *ikuyas*?

What is going on here? Maybe the answers can be found within the DMT experience itself?

CHAPTER 11
THE CHEMICAL LIMINALS

Earlier I suggested that, for most of us, pre-pubescence and old age are the usual times that we can escape "Plato's cave" (see p146). However, this idea may need qualifying. There is growing evidence that there are other circumstances that allow us to break out of the analogue telephone system which is neurologically facilitated Kenoma and tune into the glial-cell-facilitated Pleroma. These circumstances may be brought about by the perception-altering substances known by the collective term psychedelics. Many psychedelics are found in the natural world as outcomes of molecular activity and plant evolution. They can change totally how a perceiving entity encounters the phenomenal realm.

In an effective updating of Plato's cave allegory, philosopher Joseph Bicknell makes the following observation:

> … ordinary perception can be likened to staring at reflections in the surface of a perfectly still pool of water (the mind) where the surface of the pool is invisible. The reflections remain perfectly solid and convincing/realistic so long as the surface of the water/mind is undisturbed. The psychedelic trip-effect is like causing a splash in the water so that the surface is distorted and becomes visible; the reflections then ripple, undulate and fragment, and reveal themselves to be mere reflections as opposed to being the actual things they reflect.[1]

Bicknell is referring here to the way in which perception-altering psychedelics can "cleanse" Blake's "Doors of Perception" and allow the prisoner to escape the cave.

The word "psychedelic" is taken from the Greek words *psychē* ("soul") and *dēloun* ("to make visible", "to reveal"). Interestingly, the author of the Blake-inspired book *The Doors of Perception*, Aldous Huxley, suggested an alternative word: *phanerothyme*. This has the same Greek source as "Phaneron". *Phaneros* is Greek for "manifest" and *thymos* for "spirit". Huxley discussed this terminology with psychiatrist Humphry Osmond after his experiences with mescaline, one of the original mind-expanding drugs. In a letter to Osmond he wrote:

> To make this mundane world sublime,
> Take half a gram of phanerothyme.

Osmond, in similar poetic fashion, replied:

> To fathom Hell or soar angelic,
> Just take a pinch of psychedelic.[2]

It was LSD (lysergic acid diethylamide) that broke through into public consciousness in the mid 1960s, but in recent years the focus of attention has been on another substance, N, N-Dimethyltryptamine, usually known by its acronym DMT.

What is DMT?

It is generally believed that the most powerful, and certainly most intriguing, of all psychedelic substances is N, N-Dimethyltryptamine (DMT). This simple organic molecule is found in many animals and probably all plants with the exception of fungus (fungi have their own variation, 4-HO-DMT). Curiously, DMT has not been found in insects: why this is so is a genuine mystery, particularly as many DMT entities encountered seem to have distinctly "insectoid" features.

So what exactly is DMT and why does it seem to act as a conduit to alternative realities?

In 1955 an article was published in the *Journal of the American Chemical Society* by a small team of analytical chemists, Fish, Johnson and Horning.[3] This group was keen to understand the hallucinogenic elements of the snuff known as *cohoba*, used by the indigenous peoples of the Caribbean and the Orinoco basin of South America. It was known that the source of *cohoba* was *Anadenanthera peregrina*, a tree native to that area. The researchers discovered two substances that may have been responsible for the powerful effects. The most likely, they concluded, was an alkaloid named bufotenin. Alkaloids are naturally occurring organic compounds that impact the perceptual centres of the brain with varying degrees of intensity. One of the earliest discovered was morphine in 1804. This was soon followed by xanthine (1817), strychnine (1818), atropine (1819), quinine (1820), caffeine (1820), nicotine (1828) and cocaine (1860). Bufotenin was isolated from toad skin during World War I.

It is not surprising that the team thought that bufotenin was the psychoactive element in *cohoba*. Images of toads in Mesoamerican art suggested that the connection had long been known by the indigenous peoples of that area. They therefore dismissed the role of the other substance, which was DMT.

A couple of years before, in 1953, a Hungarian chemist named Stephan Szára was planning a study into the causes of schizophrenia. He had heard of the profound effects of LSD and was keen to procure a small supply for his own experiments. At that time the only source of the drug was the Sandoz Laboratory in Switzerland. Because he lived behind the Iron Curtain, and was a citizen of a country potentially hostile to the West, his request was refused. He had to find an alternative psychoactive substance to continue his work. Initially he tried mescaline, which he managed to order from the UK. He experimented with this on himself and was pleased with the results. On reading the Fish et al. paper in 1955, Szára decided to try and synthesise DMT for himself. He suspected that the psychoactive ingredient in *cohoba* was not bufotenine but DMT. Fortunately for him, in the previous year American chemists ME Speeter and WC Anthony had published a paper outlining a method whereby DMT could be synthesized.

Using this process and his own knowledge of organic chemistry, he was able to create 10 grams of pure DMT. He decided to orally ingest 250 micrograms of the substance. He was disappointed when nothing happened. But undeterred, and somewhat bravely, he increased the dose over a period of days to 10mg (about three quarters of a gram). Still nothing happened. It was then that an associate suggested he inject directly into a vein. This he did in April 1956. He found that 30 mg elicited mild symptoms such as pupil dilation and the perception of coloured geometric forms. He increased the dose to 75 mg and within three minutes had a full DMT experience.

As soon as he had recovered from his intravenously facilitated encounter, Szára realized he had discovered a new hallucinogen.

Keen to test it, he set up the first study of the effects of the substance at the National Institute for Mental and Nervous Diseases in Budapest. He worked with 30 volunteers, all of whom received 50 mg injected into a muscle. This was when the "entities" introduced themselves. Here is how one volunteer described her experience:

> The whistling has stopped; I have arrived. In front of me are two quiet, sunlit Gods. They gaze at me and nod in a friendly manner. I think they are welcoming me into this new world.[4]

This had not been expected. Szára and his associates had no interest in speculating on the true nature of these seemingly independent beings, even though similar encounters were reported by other volunteers. This is how he later described his approach:

> When these experiences, such as God, strange creatures and other worldliness [*sic*], appeared in our DMT studies, we did not philosophize about them but, as psychiatrists, we simply classified them as hallucinations.[5]

Of course, as I discussed in my book *Opening the Doors of Perception*, science uses the term "hallucination" to dismiss any experiences that it cannot even begin to explain. Indeed, even today, in the second decade of the 21st century, neurologists still have no idea what hallucinations actually are and why the mind creates them.

Why did the first experiencer call the entities "Gods"? This is a strange interpretation. Psychologist Dr David Luke of the University of Greenwich, London, suggests this could be because some entities encountered in DMT states have an air of supreme authority. Luke points to similarities between the Szára volunteers' experiences with encounters described by later adventurers into the DMT realm. For example, take this quotation from the online Serendipity website:

> I did see intelligent insect alien god beings who explained that they had created us, and were us in the future, but that [this] was all taking place outside of linear time.[6]

As we shall see, Dr Luke has had his own experiences with entities which actually claim godlike provenance.

DMT researcher Anton Bilton describes how, when he was 15 years old, he found himself capable of, as he terms it, "astral travelling". Note that this was not an exogenously DMT-facilitated experience but a state that spontaneously occurred during a school day mid-morning break. He considers this to be "the most profound experience in my life". Such was the impact of the experience that he has spent the rest of his life seeking ways to contact the entities he encountered.

Bilton finds the motivations of the entities he has encountered over the years quite puzzling. Some are kind, some indifferent, but some are also malevolent and seem to wish him harm. He describes an encounter with a monstrous, ten-foot-tall demon which screamed these words at him:

> You, you ignorant humans, … what I do as archdestroyer.[7]

This incident is far from unique. In the early 1960s anthropologist Michael Harner undertook a field trip to Amazonia. He was interested in the culture and beliefs of the Conibo people of Peru. He found their worldview confusing and started asking some deep questions, whereupon the elders told him that to fully understand he needed to drink ayahuasca. Hesitantly, he decided this was the only route to follow. Within a few minutes he found himself in what he described as a "celestial cavern". He saw various entities, many of which were hybrids of humans and birds – creatures similar to those depicted on the walls of ancient Egyptian tombs. But what happened next seems to be of greatest significance with regard to our own enquiry.

Harner felt that he was dying and called for assistance from the Conibo shamans who were facilitating his ayahuasca journey. Help came in the most peculiar way. He was shown that his visions were being created by, as he later described them,

> giant reptilian creatures reposing sluggishly at the lowermost depths of the back of my brain, where it met the top of the spinal column. I could only vaguely see them in what seemed to be gloomy, dark depths.[8]

Once direct contact with them had been made, the reptilian entities told him that the information they were about to share with him was reserved for the dying and the dead. He then saw, projected in front of him, how the reptilians had come to Earth eons ago, fleeing from something out in space. He was then shown how these beings created life on this planet in order to hide within it and not be discovered by whatever was seeking them. What he was then told is really intriguing. The dragon-like entities informed him that they were inside all forms of life, including humans, who are but the receptacles and servants of these creatures. Indeed, this was exactly how this message was being conveyed to him – information being sent from deep within his own cellular structure.[9]

After Harner had recovered from his ayahuasca experience, he felt uneasy. If the serpents were to be believed, the knowledge he had been given was only for the "dying and the dead". He decided he needed to share this with his countrymen. He set off in a dugout canoe with an outboard motor attached toward a local American evangelist mission a few miles away downriver. On arrival, he explained to one of the missionary couples what he had been told. The missionaries immediately became excited and grabbed hold of a Bible lying nearby. From this they read out a section in the Book of Revelation (12.7):

And there was war in heaven: Michael and his angels fought against the dragon; and the dragon fought and his angels. And prevailed not; neither was their place found any more in heaven. And the great dragon was cast out, that old serpent, called the Devil, and Satan, which deceiveth the whole world: he was cast out into the earth, and his angels were cast out with him.

I am surprised that the missionaries failed to make a link, as we have done earlier, with the Book of Enoch, but I suppose the reason is simply that the book of Enoch is not one of the authorized books of the Bible.

Harner slept the rest of the day at the mission but next day decided to head back to the Conibo village to gain more information about his encounter with the "dragons". On his return he engaged a blind old shaman in conversation. He explained to the old man that in his ayahuasca experience he had seen "giant bats" that said they were the true masters of the world. Smiling, the old shaman replied:

Oh, they're always saying that. But they are only the Masters of Outer Darkness.[10]

In early 1985 Canadian anthropologist Jeremy Narby, a 25-year-old graduate student from Stanford University, reported an uncannily similar encounter. Narby had been doing field research in the Pichis Valley in Peruvian Amazonia when he heard about the powerful hallucinations created by ayahuasca. After initially doubting the claims made, he decided to try the brew for himself. Under the guidance of an *ayahuasquero* named Ruperto Gomez, he swallowed a small cupful of the foul-tasting liquid and after a few light hallucinations found himself deeply submerged in the ayahuasca universe. What happened next changed his life. He saw, surrounding him, two gigantic boa constrictors that seemed to him to be around 50 feet (just over 15 metres) long. In his notes, recorded immediately after his experience, he wrote:

These enormous snakes are there, my eyes are closed and I see a spectacular world of brilliant lights, and in the middle of these hazy thoughts, the snakes start talking to me without words. They explain that I am just a human being. I feel my mind crack, and in the fissures, I see the bottomless arrogance of my presuppositions.[11]

So what is the true nature of these entities? Do they have actual reality outside the mind of the observer or is there something far more complex taking place? You will recall that Aleister Crowley, in his book *Magick in Theory and Practice*, suggested that whether the entities were objectively real or not was "immaterial": what was important, he argued, was the *results* of such encounters.

Later in the Luke book, the panel discusses whether the entities are analogous with shepherds, with ourselves being simply their "flock". This is a disturbing idea, because it suggests that we are, to them, a source of something useful. In his own research, discussed earlier (p99), American paranormal researcher Paul Eno had argued that many if not all entities (he was focusing on poltergeists and related non-human intelligences) are psychic vampires – a term actually used by the panel at one stage.

David Luke's interest in egregorial entities is not simply grounded in dispassionate scientific research: he is motivated too by a need to explain his own experiences with god-like entities.

In a 2008 article entitled "Disembodied Eyes Revisited: An Investigation into the Ontology of Entheogenic Entity Encounters", Luke makes some fascinating observations. He opens this paper by quoting Dr John C Lilly, the researcher whose revolutionary work we have discussed (p153). Lilly wondered how a person can differentiate between in-sanity and out-sanity. Luke interprets this question in clear-cut terms: how can one really know what is real and what is unreal when both perceptions are presented to consciousness by the same brain?

A short time before the writing of the article, Luke had taken 40 or 50 full doses of DMT, and during his experiences he had encountered a variety of extraordinary entities. In this regard he quotes renowned "psychonaut" Terence McKenna, who once said, "You get elves, everybody does." But he felt that there was much more than this to this other world, something that seemed real:

Sometimes I saw unknown god-like beings, sometimes shape-shifting mischievous imps – but increasingly I kept getting the feeling I was intruding upon a cosmic gathering to which I wasn't invited. Occasionally the effects failed to go any further than an ego-dissolution and a swim through a fractal explosion of pulsing light with the usual wild array of colors. Yet I often felt as though I was being blocked from whatever lurked beyond these multiple geometric dimensions, as well as not being allowed to revisit places to which I had been previously. A couple of times I felt so uninvited and intimidated by the entities I met that I did not wish to return, regardless of my curiosity.[12]

On his last DMT session before writing the article, Luke had smoked a full dose on a secluded beach on the river Ganges in India. On arrival in the Pleroma, he felt he had caught the entities by surprise: they were not expecting him. Possibly because of this unannounced arrival, he was able to glimpse something he should not have seen. On returning to the Kenoma, he could not recall what this had been, but he knew at the deepest level of his subconscious that he had taken a "brief glance at something truly forbidden".

The creature he had encountered in this trip was a sea of swirling eyeballs attached to snake bodies. He had the overpowering feeling that this being was a single entity. Over a period of years, he managed to put together in his own mind what he had seen that day by the Ganges. He recalled a long, sublimated dream in which he had encountered Asrael, the Islamic angel of death. He knew this because the angel told him his name. Luke adds that this was quite strange, because he had never heard of it before, encountering the name only after the dream. He then researched what Azrael was supposed to look like. To his surprise he found that according to Islamic writings Azrael has 10,000 eyes. Further research uncovered that according to the Western African Hausa civilization, the god of death also has a multitude of eyes. His name is Azrail.

Several years later events were to take an intriguing, some would say disturbing, turn. Luke, quite by accident, whilst reading a book on Tibetan magic, came across an ancient deity known as Za (or gza'). On further investigation he found that

Za appeared to humans as a being with 1,000 eyes attached to the body of a snake. Za, and his associated deities, known as the *Lu* or *Lhamayin*, were the guardians of the liminal world where our world (what I call Kenoma) overlaps with the world of the spirits (Pleroma).

After further reading of the works of noted Czech Tibetologists Rene Nebesky-Wojkowitz and Stephan Beyer, he began to believe that there had been some objective reality in his encounter with Azrael/Za. Soon afterwards he read a 1994 article by DMT experiencer Peter Meyer. Here Meyer quoted one of his associates:

> I noticed what seemed to be an opening into a large space, like looking through a cave opening to a starry sky. As I approached this I saw that resting in the opening was a large creature, with many arms, somewhat like an octopus, and all over the arms were eyes, mostly closed, as if the creature were asleep or slumbering. As I approached it the eyes opened, and it/they became aware of me. It did not seem especially well-disposed towards me, as if it did not wish to be bothered by a mere human, and I had the impression I wasn't going to get past it, so I did not try.[13]

Luke was, quite naturally, amazed. Here was another person encountering in a DMT experience what seems to be an identical entity to the one he had encountered. Not only that but the being seemed to be barring entry to another place, in the same way that Azrael/Za did in his trip.

Luke then found more articles describing the same or very similar entities populating DMT, LSD and psilocybin experiences. He comments:

> There seemed to be at least a degree of objective reality to all these reports (including mine), because they had

historical precedent, shared experience, and – most importantly – some apparent meaning.[14]

So what does this tell us? Here we have a well-respected British academic suggesting that maybe these entities have some form of independence and motivation beyond that of the observer/perceiver. This is very much the position taken by the above-mentioned Peter Meyer in his collection of "apparent communications" with DMT-induced entities.

Earlier we discussed in some detail how UFO abductions regularly involve the experiencer suffering disturbing and sometimes painful medical-related experiments. This has echoes of the dismembering elements of the shamanic journey. It is hugely significant that similar themes can be found in DMT experiences. Here one of Meyer's associates describes how the "elves" worked on him:

> I found myself once again in the company of the "elves",
> as the focus of their attention and ministrations, but they
> appeared much less colorful and altogether preoccupied
> with the task at hand, ie pouring a golden, viscous liquid
> through a network of long, intertwining, transparent
> conduits which led into the middle of my abdomen.[15]

Can a link be made between the DMT encounters and the historic and naturally created egregorial encounters described in the last chapter? I believe there can be: it is the tiny organ we have already discussed in passing, the pineal gland.

The pineal portal

All through our discussions about encounters with Egregorials, one constant seems to occur again and again, and this is the role of caves, grottoes and running water. Why is it that entrances to the inner earth should feature in this way? Of course, one could simply suggest that for our ancestors, and indeed for many of us today, caves are mysterious and even frightening. They are dark and suggest a link with another reality, known as the "chthonic". But one could easily reverse this logic and state that such fears are generated because the Other has been regularly encountered in these dark, dank places for millennia.

Why is it that our Upper Paleolithic ancestors chose caves to depict their encounters with Egregorials, with echoes of Graham Hancock's therianthropes (see p13)? Surely, in order to execute any form of work of art, illumination is needed; and yet these artists decided to create their work in the deep, virtually inaccessible caves that had no natural light. They would have needed either to have fires burning continually to illuminate the cave walls or else a complex set of mirrors to reflect any natural light to the site of depiction. Would it not have been easier to paint the images just inside the cave entrance? Yes, but this is not what they did. It seems that for them it was a case of the darker, the better.

You will recall how the Kogi people of northern Columbia have their young trainee shamans (the *mammas*) live for years in a cave environment, only brought out at night to interface with the rest of the tribe. In Islamic cultures, as we have seen (p42), the Egregorials are known as the *djinn*, a word that literally means "hidden from sight" in Arabic. They exist in darkness. Many encounters with religious figures such as the Blessed Virgin Mary also take place in caves or grottoes and, even more interestingly, the accounts often feature springs or running water. We also know from historical reports that elementals such as the Irish Tuatha De Danann were banished to live in the "hollow hills", another underground, chthonic place of darkness. This underground of elemental entities is yet another cultural universal, found across most cultures across the globe. Like shamanism itself, the belief seems to be hardwired into human belief systems.

Then we have egregorial encounters that take place late at night, usually in the darkness of a bedroom. The person seems to wake up and encounters dark, brooding figures in the room, or an entity sitting on their chest, preventing them from moving. You will recall my mother's encounter with the "grey" in exactly these circumstances.

Why is this? Why is darkness – deep Stygian darkness – associated with Egregorials?

The clue may lie in another set of beliefs which, on first evaluation, seem to have no relationship with darkness and nocturnal visitations: the preoccupation with snakes deep within the brain. The Australian Aboriginals have a concept known as the Rainbow Snake, a process by which a snake, or a number of snakes, are placed deep inside an initiate shaman's brain in order to facilitate shamanic skills. You will recall the comment made to psychologist Benny Shanon by the ice-cream vendor in the Peruvian jungle in which God decided to "put my secrets in the inner sanctum of man's own mind. Then only those who really deserve it will be able to get to it."[16]

This "inner sanctum" may be another term for the pineal gland. We need now to return our attention to this tiny organ and, more importantly, to what it has the potential to do.

Western science is convinced that consciousness, or more specifically self-aware consciousness, is a product of brain processing. The person reading these words is simply a collection of electrical charges "manifesting" in the neurons the brain. However, as Australian philosopher David Chalmers has pointed out, this model has a huge problem. How can an amalgamation of inanimate molecules and similarly inanimate electrons bring about self-aware consciousness? How can "manifest" particles create the non-manifest inner world of thoughts, dreams, ambitions and personality? He calls this the "Hard Problem", and it is clear that our present paradigm simply cannot solve it.

However, recent discoveries have suggested that the brain is not merely a classical biochemical system but something far more complex: a "macroscopic quantum system" that functions by drawing up information from a fascinating new form of energy known as "zero point". But what is even more pertinent, according to the work of Winkler and Proeckl (see pp126–8), is that this energy manifests itself as light.

Zero point energy is a consequence of the Heisenberg Uncertainty Principle. This states that if we know the position of a subatomic particle, we cannot know its speed; and if we know its speed, we cannot know its position. If a particle were at rest, we would know both. However, such particles can never be at rest, not even at absolute zero, the coldest state known to science. This is minus 273.15 degrees Celsius – three degrees below the temperature of the vacuum of space. Why this is significant is that there should be no energy at absolute zero, but there is. All space is absolutely filled to the brim with this quantum vacuum energy. This energy exists, as all energy does, within a field. Not surprisingly this is called the "zero point field" or ZPF.[17]

This idea has interesting parallels with ancient Chinese philosophy, which suggests that there is no such thing as empty space. For philosophers such as Chang Tsai, the bedrock of reality is ch'i. Ch'i translates as "gas" or "ether" and is a tenuous and non-perceptible form of matter which is present throughout space and can condense into solid material objects.

The idea that matter somehow condenses out of ch'i is amazingly prescient, because there is a process that echoes perfectly this most ancient of ideas. This fascinating new form of matter, called Bose-Einstein Condensation, was first predicted by Indian physicist Satyendra Nath Bose, who was brought up within the Eastern rather than the Western philosophical tradition. In a paper he sent to Albert Einstein in 1924, he described how it may be that if particles were cooled to a few degrees above absolute zero, they would change from being a single particle to being a collection of particles that act as if they were one.[18] Such a bizarre idea was proved when the first Bose-Einstein condensate was created in 1995 at the University of Colorado. Many years before, in 1938, a similar phenomenon was observed when a substance called helium 4 was found to have absolutely no viscosity, which meant that it could flow with absolutely no loss of energy.[19]

In principle, what is happening is that all the particles within the condensate have become one, a single particle spread out in space and time. These condensates pull their energy directly out of the ZPF in the form of zero point energy. Actually, many of us use a Bose- Einstein condensate when we listen to music using a CD player. The information from the disk is read using a laser beam, and a laser beam is technically coherent light – a beam in which all the light particles (photons) are sharing a single "coherent" state.

However, there is another application of laser technology that has direct reference to the workings of the human brain: the hologram.

Holograms are three-dimensional images created by using lasers to "photograph" an object and then reproduce the subsequent image by illuminating it with another set of lasers. This is again an application of coherent light in which a seemingly solid image can be reproduced from stored information. In 1986 two Japanese researchers, Isuki Hirano and Atsushi Hirai, suggested that coherent light is generated in vast quantities by tiny structures found deep within the neurons of the brain.[20] These structures, known as "microtubules", are so small that it is possible that the energy they use to generate the coherent light is zero point energy drawn directly from the ZPF. In other words, they draw energy from what Indian traditional philosophy called the Akashic Record and what Chang Tsai knew as ch'i.

If Hirano and Hirai are correct, then the Akashic data can be reassembled using laser-like coherent light to create seemingly three-dimensional holographic images of the stored information. This would create in the mind of the experiencer a three-dimensional version of the recording that would be totally lifelike in every way. Like the illusionary world of the *Matrix* movies, it would be indistinguishable from the "real" thing. I use speech marks here because such a model suggests that the "reality" we take for granted that is external to our bodies and supplied to us by our senses may not be as "real" as we believe. Indeed, modern neurology tells us that what we take to be external reality is a construct of the brain modelled out of the electrochemical information supplied to it from our senses.

The question is: is there a portal within the brain whereby the riches of the Akasha can be accessed? Recent discoveries have suggested that an intriguing hallucinogenic substance may be excreted by the pineal gland. If this is the case, then the body itself creates the neurochemical circumstances whereby consciousness can delve deeply into its own "inner space" and there encounter a reality wrapped within a greater reality.

To appreciate how this process works, we need to understand how the brain sends messages from one cell to another using a collection of fascinating chemicals called neurotransmitters.

Neurotransmitters are released by a neuron (brain) cell to stimulate other neurons in its vicinity, and in the process transmit impulses from one cell to the other. In turn, this facilitates the transfer of messages throughout the whole nervous system. The site where neurons meet is called the synapse. Each synapse consists of the axon terminal (transmitting end) of one cell and the dendrite (receiving end) of the next. A microscopic gap called a synaptic cleft exists between the two neurons. When a nerve impulse arrives at the axon terminal of one cell, a chemical substance is released through the membrane close to the synapse. This substance then travels across the gap in a matter of milliseconds to arrive at the postsynaptic membrane of the adjoining neuron. This chemical release is stimulated by the electrical activity of the cell. Across the other side of the cleft, at the end of the receiving dendrite, are specialized areas that act as docking areas for particular neurotransmitters. These are known as "receptors". It is useful to visualize the receptors like docks at a port. Sometimes they will be open, letting in ships containing cargo, and sometimes they will be closed, with the result that some ships cannot unload their goods.

If the newly arrived neurotransmitter chemical is allowed into the dock, it is free to "instruct" the dendrite to send a particular signal along to its nucleus, then out to its own axons. When it does this, it is said to be "excitatory". Sometimes the effect of the neurotransmitter(s) released by the pre-synaptic axon is to inhibit rather than excite the post-synaptic dendrite. In this case it is said to be "inhibitory". In terms of our ship metaphor, this is when the dock is closed and cargo cannot be unloaded.

Since their first discovery in the 1930s, 50 or so neurotransmitters have been found, the most important being serotonin, noradrenaline, glutamate and a group of pain-killing opiates called endorphins. Only after 1972, when Nobel Prize-winning chemist Julius Axelrod made a surprising discovery, was it believed that DMT might belong somehow with this group.

In a routine test of some brain material, Axelrod found traces of DMT. This chemical is a member of the amine family. Seven years earlier another amine had been found in human blood. This was, in itself, a surprise, as until then amines had only been found in the cells of invertebrates. The discovery of an amine in the brain was a total puzzle. It was believed that these chemicals had no function within the human body. So why was there DMT in the brain?

In 2001 a new family of receptor cells was discovered. Called trace amine-associated receptors (TAARs), these cells were like locks in which only one key could be used, and that key was an amine. What this suggested was startling: that amines are a form of neurotransmitter.[21] As DMT is a form of amine, then its reason for being in the brain was clear: it is there because the brain is designed to work with it.

Some scientists believe there is one specific site in the brain where DMT is produced: the pineal gland. One of the major proponents of this argument is Dr Rick Strassman of the University of New Mexico.

Indeed, Strassman has further suggested that DMT may be responsible for the near-death experience itself.[22] Could this be the link that has long been sought: that the light experience reported by virtually all who have reported an NDE is generated by the release of DMT within the brain? If so, how might this work?

Earlier we saw how it may be possible for consciousness to access information directly from the zero point field, also known as the Akashic Record or simply "ch'i". The energy contained within this field, zero point energy, can be perceived as light in the same way that electromagnetic energy is perceived. We know from the work of Winkler and Proeckl that the stimulation of the pineal gland by the modulated light of Lucia can generate within the "mind's eye" an "inner light" of profound intensity.

Could it be that the facilitator of this "inner light" may be an internally generated version of DMT? There is sufficient evidence for researchers to pursue this possibility through empirical research. If DMT is one day found to have a crucial involvement in the workings of the brain, then we may have the start of a working model of how consciousness can perceive two forms of light: the light of our everyday waking world that illuminates everything we see; and an inner light that is drawn up from the depths of the quantum world and illuminates our *inner* universe.

However, in presenting this model we end up with a big question: which of these two "illuminated" realities is real and which one is an illusion? Or are they both aspects of a greater reality? Are we, as John C Lilly asked, In-Sane or Out-Sane, or both at once?

I would now like to return to my mother's experience with the "grey". You will recall that it happened very early one morning: it was dark and she believed she had just woken up. It is clear from her description that she was in a state of sleep paralysis, brought about by the release of melatonin. Could it be that within the darkness her brain was releasing internally generated (endogenous) DMT and that this facilitated her awareness of the mysterious entity?

Could this be why caves are so important in egregorial encounters? Time and time again in this book we have been presented with stories of beings that dwell in caverns or grottos. We have the tales of the djinn coming up from the Underworld, the Tuatha De Dannan hiding in their tumuli and various versions of the Blessed Virgin Mary being seen at the entrances to caves. Is this all simply coincidence? The idea that darkness contains dangerous creatures may be more than a simple race-memory involving bears and sabre-toothed tigers. It may be rooted in human physiology.

So what evidence is there for my suggestion that darkness stimulates the pineal gland to synthesize endogenous DMT from the already-discussed "hormone of darkness", melatonin?

Independent researcher Beach Barrett, based in North Carolina in the USA, is one of the most original thinkers in the field of the pineal gland and endogenous DMT production. In his paper "METAtonin Research: An Introduction to METAtonin, the Pineal Gland Secretion That Helps Us Access Higher Understanding", he presents his own theory on what may be taking place in the brain during higher states of consciousness whereby Egregorials are encountered.

DMT is biosynthesized from tryptamine by the actions of an enzyme called indolethylamine N-methyltransferase (IMMT). Barrett suggests that when the pineal gland secretes IMMT, it catalyses two methyl groups to combine with a tryptamine molecule. This results in the creation of a DMT-rich variation of melatonin that he calls METAtonin.

Because of the unique location of the pineal gland, any endogenously created METAtonin is not deactivated by the actions of monoamine oxidase (MAO-A) as it is in the gut. You will recall that the reason why ayahuasca is so effective is that it is a mixture of two plants, *Banisteriopsis caapi* and *Psychotria viridis*, one of which contains DMT while the other acts as an inhibitor of MAO-A. The more the effectiveness of

MAO-A can be minimized, then the greater the effect DMT has on consciousness.

According to Barrett, METAtonin, once activated, creates a new neural pathway within the brain. A series of linked neurons are actively stimulated in a particular sequence, creating a new circuit. This in turn evolves into a consciousness feedback loop, similar to a hyperlink in a computer program. This may also stimulate other areas of the body known to create DMT – for example, the thyroid gland and the lungs.

In an intriguing suggestion, Barrett proposes that the release of METAtonin creates sleep paralysis, the incredibly common mysterious state of egregorial awareness we have touched upon a number of times (see pp135–137). Sleep paralysis is brought about because METAtonin and melatonin are active at the same time within the bloodstream. The melatonin deactivates the ability of the body to move in REM sleep, whereas the METAtonin actively wakes up consciousness.

In support of his case Barrett suggests that METAtonin is found in high concentrations in the blood of embryos and children up to the age of three, adding that the concentration increases again at the point of death and in doing so brings about the well-documented phenomenon of near-death experience. However, it is the early childhood experiences that particularly interest Barrett. He points out that the pineal gland first appears in the human embryo at the 49th day after conception. At this time, it is located at the back of the throat and then slowly moves upwards until it arrives at its final location in the centre of the brain. He suggests that this may leave a small duct which may, under certain conditions, leak METAtonin into the back of the throat. He points out that there are certain Eastern texts that refer to something known as the "nectar of sublime awareness".

Could Barrett's model explain Halliday's "Invizikids" phenomenon? Certainly it can for infant encounters and, if the effect of METAtonin creation only gradually declines over a period of years, it could explain childhood encounters as well.

Yet there is another link between endogenous DMT and sleep paralysis.

In controlled experiments it has been discovered that a DMT-like substance, bufotenine (5-Hydroxy-DMT), can create in its experiencers a feeling of constriction in the throat and pressure on the chest, which in turn brings about a sensation of deep anxiety. This is exactly what is reported in cases of sleep paralysis.

So our model seems to have a degree of explanatory power. But to really join the dots we need a deeper and broader analysis of the science behind the perceptions. Let us now, in the following chapter, trace our final pathway to the egregorial universe.

CHAPTER 12
EGREGORIAL SCIENCE

What do we mean when we say something is "real"? For example, is the Taj Mahal a "real" building? We have evidence that it exists three-dimensionally from photographs or from a process similar to photography (sight, while walking around it). In both cases an image is created by particles (or, as we shall discover soon, waves) of electromagnetic energy stimulating a chemical reaction on light-sensitive film or on the light-sensitive rods and cones of the eye's retina. Anyone fortunate enough to travel to Agra can walk up to the Taj and touch it. But, as we shall see, at no time in this process of touching is the person actually in physical contact with the surface of the building: electrostatic fields ensure that no contact is ever made.

Our so-called proof of the reality of the Taj is the fact that other people agree that the Taj is there in three-dimensional space. Moreover, we all agree with what it looks like.

Now, was Queen Victoria real? The only evidence we have of her existence is photographs and old film. She no longer "exists", so does that mean she is no longer "real"?

Using the same logic, is Sherlock Holmes real? He is not here in the same way that Queen Victoria is not here. But we also believe that he was a creation of the imagination of Arthur Conan Doyle, who is also not here any more. Most people in the English-speaking world will recognize an image of Sherlock Holmes – probably a similar number to those who would recognize an image of Queen Victoria.

So what about fairies or alien "greys"? These entities offer great challenges to our powers of reasoning and logic, largely because some people doubt whether anyone has experienced them as a phenomenon.

By the latest count, modern physics (the Standard Model) has 48 "point particles" (that is, particles that have no substance that extends in space: they have no left or right sides). However, they have mass. How can this be? How can a billion point particles come together and create something that has extension? Surely, zero multiplied by a billion is still zero.

These point particles, in turn, need invisible "fields" in which to function. At the present time, we know of four of these invisible force fields These invisible fields need carrier-particles to spread the field through space (in a vacuum or otherwise). These carrier-particles are *virtual*, in that they too can never be observed, as they are created and destroyed in an instant (that is, in no time). The location in which these virtual particles "exist" is space. Space is a mystery because we do not know what it actually is. If it had no particles in it (virtual or otherwise), would it be anything? Space is not the distance between objects, because if those objects disappeared, so would space itself. And is not space related directly to time. So with no objects in *space-time,* then space and time cease to exist.

For the record, the 17 point particles are: 6 quarks (up, down, charm, strange, bottom and top), gluon, photon, electron, muon, muon-neutrino, tau, tau-neutrino, W-boson, Z-boson, electron-neutrino, Higgs boson. The four "forces" are gravity, the weak nuclear force, the strong nuclear force and electromagnetism. These forces are known as "non-contact forces", in that they can act on objects without ever coming in contact with them. Gravity is the force of attraction between all bodies that have mass: it is proportional to the mass of the first body times the mass of the second body divided by the square of the distance between them. Electromagnetism is the force that causes interactions between electrically charged particles: it has various manifestations such as electricity, magnetism, radio waves and visible light. The strong nuclear force only works at a very short distance: it is active within the nucleus of an atom. The weak nuclear force mediates the beta decay by which a neutron decays into a proton and, in doing so, creates a beta particle and a neutrino.

These forces need carriers to transfer the force from one location to another ("spooky action at a distance", as Einstein termed it). A good analogy is when a large object like a medicine ball is thrown from one person to another. The thrower imparts a "force" by throwing the ball, which causes the catcher to recoil with the impact. The medicine ball is, in this case, the "carrier" of the force from one object to another. These force carriers are known as "bosons". For electromagnetism, the boson is the photon. For the strong force it is the gluon; and for the weak force it is the Z-boson.

And that is about it. Everything that is seemingly real in the physical world is created out of countless point particles, all of which have no extension in space. So the question we need to ask is, how can countless bits of nothing create anything? What is really "out there"?

Let me return to the idea (expressed in my Taj Mahal example) that we never actually physically touch anything in the external environment. When we feel something, the sensation of touching is, in fact, caused by the repelling force of the negatively charged atoms in our hands (or skin) and the negatively charged atoms in the object being touched. Similarly, we "see" the world through electromagnetic energy, in the form of light, hitting our retina and being converted into electrochemical signals which propagate using potassium ions along the neurons in the brain and ultimately arrive at the visual cortex. Of course, the "carriers" of the electromagnetic "wave" are particles known as "photons". The stream of particles (or the wave) travels at exactly the speed of light and, in doing so, from its relative point of view, exists in a timeless location. Similarly, these photons have zero mass so you can place together as many as you like, even an infinite number of them, and you will still not have anything that is physically located in space.

In sum, any perception of "reality" is mediated by things that literally do not exist in space or time. This speed of light example can also be applied to the propagation of the electromagnetic field. It exists in a timeless place. To this you can add the theory of relativity: the idea that every viewpoint is equally valid and that electromagnetic energy *always* travels at the speed of light relative to the observer, irrespective of the observer's speed in relation to other observers and the speed of light. We learn something of profound significance about the "observer" when we discuss the idea that subatomic particles (including photons) are brought into existence by the very act of observation.

The intriguing point here is that our understanding of the workings of the physical, as outlined above, is based upon a premise that is invalidated by the very things it has discovered. Welcome to the illusion that is materialist reductionism.

The contradiction of materialist-reductionism

Modern Western science has been based upon the same basic principle for more than 300 years. With the Enlightenment came an approach to understanding the inner workings of the material world by which materials and processes were broken down (reduced) to their component parts. By being subjected to this process, they could be understood. For example, if I were an alien visitor to Earth and I discovered a motorcycle I could, by taking it apart, attempt to understand its functioning and its purpose. By understanding the interactions between the various components of the motorbike, I could not only learn what it was for but could also attempt to create another motorbike.

This approach has been applied with great success to virtually everything we encounter in the physical universe. Chemistry is a wonderful example. As soon as it was realized that all physical objects can be broken down into molecules

and atoms, humanity – or, more specifically, Western science –
was able to really understand how nature worked.

This much-vaunted process is now generally believed to
be the absolutely correct position regarding the true nature
of the physical universe. I agree totally that everything we
know about the universe around us has come about through
this process. In fact, however, it provides merely a partial
answer to the fundamental questions. If we are looking for
a complete picture of the universe, we (and science) have to
accept that at its basic level, the universe is not material but
non-physical *information*. It is processed and synthesized
from information – or in-formation, to offer a suggestive
etymology.

I am going to use the materialist-reductionist process to
show just how confused this position is. Let us take a huge
mountain made of granite. You will recall from my discussion
about Dr Johnson's infamous, and totally incorrect, *agumentum
ad lapidum* ("argument from stone") right at the start of this
book (p4). We found that the lofty granite mountains we see
are made of ... nothing! It is your act of "observation", together
with every other "observing consciousness", that creates "it"
(the mountain) from "bit" (the in-formation field).

I would now like to turn to the contents of each atom
in the universe, with its electrons, protons and neutrons. It
is important to realize that every electron in the universe is
absolutely identical to every other electron, and the same goes
for every proton and every neutron. As we have seen, electrons
are elementary particles, which means that they are not made
up of any other, smaller particles (see p5). Protons and
neutrons are not elementary particles: these are made up of
smaller particles called quarks. It is these that are elementary.
So, all physical matter, when boiled down to its constituent
parts, is made up of electrons and quarks. Every proton in the
universe is actually two up quarks and one down quark. Every
neutron in the universe is one up quark and two down quarks.
So, all the matter in the physical universe is simply electrons,

down quarks and up quarks – three particles, all of which, as we have discovered, have no actual extension in space.

There is one crucial fact about all subatomic particles, and that is that if they are not "observed", they do not exist. In effect, just like our egregorial entities, they need an observing mind to bring them into "reality".

I will attempt to explain, as best I can, how such a startling conclusion can be drawn from our modern understanding of physics. Read this next section very carefully. Remember that all of it is based upon real science, not speculation or a "new age" misinterpretation of quantum physics. This is how the universe works.

Down the rabbit hole

Science has always used observation and experimentation to prove truths about the natural world. Indeed, the concept of the observer is central to a great deal of modern science. For example, the word "relativity", used so often in relation to Albert Einstein's amazing discoveries, means relative to the position of an "observer". In quantum physics something known as the "observer effect" is a crucial concept, and the "act of measurement" by an "observer" brings into existence matter in the guise of subatomic particles such as electrons, atoms and even molecules – the building blocks of the material universe. But what exactly is an "observer"? In order to understand exactly how amazing this discovery is, we need to go back and review the history of the major facilitator of any act of observation: light. Light is crucial for our perceptions of the universe. It is the reflection of light on objects in three-dimensional space that allows us to perceive those objects at a distance. But light itself, however mundane and all-pervasive it may be, is strange.

Imagine dropping a pebble into a pond. The waves form a series of ripples moving out from the point where the pebble entered the water. Now imagine what would happen if a barrier were placed across the pond. As the waves hit the barrier, they bounce back in the direction they came. Now we place two holes in the barrier, both much smaller than the wavelength of the ripples. On the other side of the barrier two sets of waves, starting at each hole, spread out as if two new pebbles were dropped in the water at the same place as each hole. As the two new sets of ripples move out, they begin to "interfere" with each other, disrupting the flow of the two sets of semicircles. In some places the two sets of ripples add up to make extra-large ripples; in other places, the two sets of ripples cancel out leaving little, or no, wave motion in the water.

The same exercise can be done with light. Light is shone through a single hole in a barrier. As the light flows out, it encounters a second barrier, this time with two holes. The light acts like a wave, in that each hole then starts its own wave pattern on the other side of the second barrier. Immediately the two waves start to interfere with each other. A screen is set up after the second barrier. When the light hits this screen, it shows a pattern of light and dark stripes. These stripes are called *interference fringes*. They correspond to where the light waves add together (*constructive interference*) and where the waves cancel each other out (*destructive interference*).

The problem then becomes how light "waves" travel in a vacuum – for example, how they manage to traverse the 93 million miles of empty space between the Sun and the Earth. In order for waves to move in any direction, they need something to wave *in*. A water wave is a disturbance within the water. As we have already discussed, when a pebble is dropped in a pond, waves move outwards from the point where the pebble entered the water. But it is the water that is waving. If there was no water, the waves would not exist. Sound waves are similar. Sound is a disturbance in the air, and it is the air that is the "medium" by which a sound reaches your ears. But in the vacuum of space there is no medium. As the famous advertising tag for the movie *Alien* stated, "In space nobody can hear you scream." Light, like sound, should have a problem in space. But it doesn't. Light reaches us from billions and billions of miles away. We see the light of stars and galaxies. So how can this be?

To explain this conundrum, it was postulated that the vacuum of space was filled by a medium known as the "lumniferous ether". It was this that carried the light waves across space. Sadly, in 1887 two American researchers, Albert A Michelson and Edward W Morley proved that space is indeed a total vacuum and that the "ether" does not exist.

Eighteen years later, in 1905, Albert Einstein solved the problem; and, in doing so, created the greatest mystery of science, one that remains a mystery even now, more than a century later. His solution was, on paper at least, a simple one: Einstein proposed that light in certain circumstances was made up of individual particles. As far as he was concerned, this was the only way that another particular puzzle for early 20th-century science could be solved. When light was shone on a solid object, it seemed to "kick out" electrons from the surface. This phenomenon, known as the "photoelectric effect", could not be explained. As Einstein said in his 1905 paper, if light is made of particles, then each particle hits the surface and knocks out the electrons. This supposition was supported by experimentation, and in recognition of this discovery Einstein was awarded the Nobel Prize for physics. One problem solved; many more created. If light could be shown to be made up of discrete packets of energy, how can this be squared with the fact that light is also a wave?

Later experimentation, using variations on the twin-slit experiment discussed above, has shown that light is *both* a wave and a particle. It depends on whether it is being observed or not. Yes, weird as it appears, that is the reality. It seems that when it is looked at, light is a particle; and when it is not being looked at, it is a wave. In effect, this means that consciousness in some way directly affects the basic nature of light.

But things have become stranger still. It been discovered that particles of "matter" – that is, the solid bits that make up our supposedly physical world – also have this strange wave-particle duality. In 1989 researcher A Tonomura and his colleagues at the Hitachi Advanced Laboratory at Gakushuin University in Tokyo found that electrons have the same duality.[1] Problematic, yes, but electrons are incredibly small and nobody has ever seen or photographed one. Atoms and molecules are different. Molecules are, in a very real sense, the building blocks of the physical world. In recent years it has been discovered that molecules – large molecules such as Buckminsterfullerene, which has 60 atoms in its structure – *come into existence* when "observed". My wording here is quite precise. Quantum physics tells us that the waves that make up physical objects such as electrons, atoms and molecules are not like water waves or sound waves. They are waves of probability and are purely mathematical structures; they have no physical reality. What makes them physically real is when their probability wave is "collapsed" by an act of observation.

Austrian physicist Anton Zeilinger and his team at the University of Vienna have now shown that even larger molecules, such as the interestingly named $C284.H190.F320.N4.S12$, which consists of 800 atoms, show wave-particle duality. This huge advance in the size of particles showing this "consciousness-effect" pushes the barrier between weird quantum behaviours ever closer to the nice, safe world of Newtonian physics, and closer toward an extremely interesting barrier: that of viruses.

Of course, there is still a great debate about what we mean by an "act of observation", in that all acts of observation are, in effect, a measurement. Traditional physicists argue that by simply being "measured" – that is, by being in contact with already collapsed matter – any wave function becomes a solid object. Others argue that an act of measurement only takes place when it is consciously evaluated by a sentient being.

The implications of this "measurement problem" are profound. If true, then we all create the reality around us by observing it. Suddenly consciousness is central to the creation of the physical world, rather than something peripheral. Is this how Egregorials can manifest in the Kenoma? Assuming that Egregorials are also conscious entities, and therefore also responsible for creating their own realities, then could it be that the overlap of consciousnesses in the "observer" and the "Egregorial" exists in some kind of feedback loop?

A possible way out of this mystery is to follow the example of the late and much-respected mathematical physicist John Wheeler and suggest that physical reality itself is not actually solid in any real sense. It is made up not of tiny bits of "stuff", but something far more intriguing: pure information.

This extraordinary conclusion was first made by a group of scientists working in Copenhagen in the 1920s. Under the leadership of the great Danish physicist Neils Bohr, these dedicated researchers devised a model of reality in which subatomic particles have a statistical "reality" that becomes actual when they are observed. Not surprisingly, this model has become known as the Copenhagen Interpretation. Such is the power of this statistical model that over the years it has become the most successful theory known to science. Not one of its predictions has been shown to be erroneous. The theory may be counterintuitive and fly in the face of common sense, but it seems to be an accurate reflection of how the universe actually works.

Earlier, I used the terms "it" and "bit" quite precisely (p186). I did so to prepare for a more detailed analysis of the subject, looking at the fascinating "it from bit" model of Professor John Archibald Wheeler.

It from Bit

John Archibald Wheeler was one of the greatest scientific minds of the late 20th century. He was a professor of physics at Princeton University from 1938 to 1976, and the director of the Center for Theoretical Physics at the University of Texas at Austin from 1976 to 1986. By the time of his death in 2008, he had returned to Princeton as a professor emeritus. It was Wheeler who explained nuclear fission in terms of quantum physics, and he was a crucial member of the Manhattan Project, exploring the potential for nuclear weapons. On a more peaceful note, it was Wheeler who first used the now popular term "black hole" to explain areas of space where the gravitational pull is so strong that not even light can escape.

Less well known is that Wheeler was a great advocate of the idea that reality is created by consciousness. In his 2004 book *Science and Ultimate Reality: Quantum Theory, Cosmology and Complexity* he wrote that "no elementary phenomenon is a phenomenon until it is a registered [observed] phenomenon.[2] Here he suggests this does not mean that the phenomenon is "created" by the act of observation, but that it has no existence until it is recorded. For Wheeler this applied to events that had already taken place in the deep past. For him the concept of "now" has no objective meaning. Indeed, many readers may be surprised to learn that such a seemingly odd idea was shared by none other than Albert Einstein. In a famous quote, he stated that "time and space are modes by which we think and not conditions by which we live."

Both Wheeler and Einstein believed that time was a concept of the conscious (observing) mind and not an external phenomenon. This is a reasonable position to take, because "time" is impossible to describe by any kind of objective generalization. Most people fall into the trap of assuming that time equals "clock time", but this is merely a hand sweeping across a clock face or the turning of digital numbers for our convenience. This is not, in itself, time: to posit the equivalence is to confuse the measurement with the measured. Time is far more elusive than that. As far as Wheeler was concerned, we exist in a permanent now where all times coexist. Time does not flow, it just is. As Wheeler wrote:

Beginning with the "Big Bang", the universe expands and cools. After eons of dynamic development, it gives rise to observership. Acts of observer-participance – via the mechanism of the delayed-choice experiment – in turn give tangible "reality" to the universe not only now but back to the beginning. To speak of the universe as a self-excited circuit is to imply once more a participatory universe ...[3]

From this Wheeler began to think about the true nature of external reality. He concluded that what we think of as solid and physical is, in fact, simply binary information that our act of observation perceives as being external to us and having an independent existence. You will note that this is a similar position to the one I have taken with regard to Egregorials. They definitely exist but they are not external to us. They are, in a real sense, brought into existence by an experience – created out of information and drawn up from the hard drive of the zero point field. Wheeler describes this in precisely chosen language:

It from Bit symbolizes the idea that every item of the physical world has at bottom – at a very deep bottom, in most instances – an immaterial source and explanation; that what we call reality arises in the last analysis from the posing of yes-no questions and the registering of equipment-evoked responses; in short, that all things physical are information-theoretic in origin and that this is a participatory universe.[4]

Note that he uses the term "participatory universe" in both quotations above. By this he means that we do not observe our universe, we participate in its creation. This applies to not only the universe as it is now but also how it has been in the past, and possibly even the future. He then adds the following extraordinary statement:

If we're ever going to find an element of nature that explains space and time, we surely have to find something that is deeper than space and time something that itself

has no localization in space and time … something
of a pure knowledge-theoretical character, an atom of
information which has no localization in between the
point of entry and the point of registration.[5]

Wheeler calculated the number of "bits" to encode "it" (the
known universe) to be 8×10^{88}.[6] This is a huge number but not
an infinitude.

Does this suggest that the Kenoma is, in fact, a form of
computer simulation? If this is the case, then nothing is
actually physical and everything we perceive, including the
Egregorials themselves, is simply (if such a word can be applied
to such a complex model) digital-reality creations, entities
created out of bits.

So where may the "bits" be found? Well, it could all be to
do with our DNA and "the snakes", as we shall soon see.

DNA and life

Francis Crick, together with James Watson, Rosalind Franklin
and Raymond Gosling, was responsible for discovering the
double-helix structure of DNA in 1953. He subsequently
became intrigued by the actual origins of this genetic code. In
his book *Life Itself: Its Origin and Nature*, published in 1962,
he suggested that DNA is such a complex organic molecule
that its origins must have been extraterrestrial. In other words,
the basis of life on this planet is an alien interloper.

Of course, how "life" itself came about is a huge mystery.
The phenomenon defies one of nature's fundamental laws:
the Second Law of Thermodynamics. This states that there
is a universal tendency toward degeneration and disorder.
This does not happen with life itself. In February 1943 Erwin
Schrödinger gave a series of lectures entitled *What is Life?*
at Trinity College Dublin. Here he argued that in order for
life to create order out of disorder, there must be another
process going on, a process involving instructions in which an

organism's design and function are encoded. This process must involve the giving and receiving of information. In 1944 the lectures were published in a book with the same title. In this book Schrödinger suggested that a new form of physics was needed to account for living matter.

That life seems to have a purpose, a motivation for change and improvement, was first elucidated by Aristotle, who created the term "teleology". This is derived from the Greek word *telos*, meaning "goal" or "end". Many centuries later, in 1885, German embryologist Hans Dreisch discovered that if one mutilated the embryo of a sea urchin, it would simply reassemble itself into the expected organic structure. It was as if some kind of blueprint was being followed, and that this was available in some mysterious way throughout the development process. The question for me in this regard is first, who or what has created the blueprint; and, no less important, who is "reading" the blueprint and acting on it? Are we to believe that there is no cognitive process going on here? If there isn't, how does each of the component parts, all working together with a final goal or outcome, become organized, unless there is a guiding force, external to them, which can physically change their actions? Dreisch was of a similar opinion and suggested the existence of a creative, directional force he called *entelechy*. This too is Greek, meaning "complete, perfect, final form". In many ways this Aristotle's teleology.

The problem was that in order for entelechy to manipulate matter, it needed to have its own form of energy, and this transfer of energy from the entelechial source and the receiving matter should be measurable.

Life itself changes the physical environment it finds itself in. It evolves out of nature and then amends nature. Science writer Paul Davies describes how inexorable natural processes can be changed when life enters the picture, citing the example of how humankind has created additional plutonium in a universe in which, until 1940, it had virtually disappeared: there are now about a thousand tons of it.

But how did life come about? There is no gradation between life and non-life. A recently dead mouse is as chemically complex as a living mouse, but we do not say that this mouse is 99.9 per cent alive. Life has gone from it. This is not a matter of degradation. Something is dead or alive, quite simply.

It is self-evident that DNA is responsible for the elaboration of life once it gets started. But herein lies another, even greater mystery. How did DNA itself "evolve" without the facilitation of its own version of a DNA code? Remember, DNA has not "evolved" in the way in which all other living things have (if, indeed, DNA can be considered to be alive): it just appeared, perfectly formed, billions of years of ago. Reflecting upon a similar aspect of evolution in 1983, astronomer Fred Hoyle made the following famous observation on the miracle of life:

> A junkyard contains all the bits and pieces of a Boeing 747, dismembered and in disarray. A whirlwind happens to blow through the yard. What is the chance that after its passage a fully assembled 747, ready to fly, will be found standing there? So small as to be negligible, even if a tornado were to blow through enough junkyards to fill the whole Universe.[7]

I am well aware of the criticism that has been levelled against this analogy, but I feel that it really gets across the strange way in which falling back on pure chance really does lead to more questions than answers. The standard critique of Hoyle's statement, one regularly cited by those who take an extreme sceptic and materialist-reductionist position, is that the analogy is not an accurate reflection of evolution. Whereas the whirlwind scenario operates purely on random chance, evolution does not. Described here is an example of single-step rather than cumulative selection: it is what is known as a "saltationary jump" (an end-product entirely unlike its starting point) and, moreover, it has a target specified in advance.

I agree totally with these points. But they are used to support an evolutionary, as opposed to creationist, point of view.

However, and this is a hugely important point, DNA is *not* the product of evolution. Indeed, DNA evolved in *exactly* the way outlined in Hoyle's analogy. It did operate via random chance, it is an example of a single-step rather than cumulative selection, a saltationary jump. DNA seems to have just spontaneously appeared out of nowhere. Although seeming to exist outside any objectives regarding its own existence, it came to facilitate an objective: to evolve ever more complex forms of life.

The oldest traces of life on Earth date back to around 3.5 billion years. Astonishingly, there is strong evidence that DNA has not changed in any way during this vast time period. Also quite amazing is that, as far as science can tell, exactly the same codes have been used since the dawn of life on this planet. The blueprint has never evolved in any way. It appeared as if from nowhere in a perfectly functional and totally effective form.

If this universe is the only one that has ever been, then the universe itself seems to have been fine-tuned for the evolution of consciousness, and now we have powerful evidence that the blueprint for life itself was similarly programmed.

It seems that life needed the development of a relationship between proteins and DNA to start on the long journey to self-referential consciousness. But the mystery is that you cannot have one without the other. As Paul Davies states:

Without a legion of proteins to fuss around it, a molecule of DNA is stranded. In simplistic terms, the job descriptions are: nucleic acids store the details about the "life plan"; proteins do the grunt work to run the organism. Both are needed. So a definition of life must take this into account.[8]

According to Davies, the solution is not just the creation of complex patterns but *supervised* and *informed* chemistry – in other words, chemistry plus *information*. In simple terms, what separates life from non-life is information. Where is this information stored? Answer: inside DNA itself!

DNA and information storage

In a series of exciting developments, it has recently been discovered that DNA works in a similar way to the kind of storage we use in modern computers. This insight has been utilized in recent years with a number of fascinating projects. For example, in 2012, George Church and a small team of researchers working at the Wyss Institute at Harvard University encoded a 53,400-word book, 11 jpg images and a JavaScript program – amounting to 5.27 million bits of data in total – into sequences of DNA.

The DNA molecule is built from organic molecules known as "nucleotides". In theory, DNA can encode two bits of data per nucleotide. These are the basic building blocks from which DNA is created. That makes 455 exabytes – roughly the capacity of 100 billion DVDs – per gram of single-stranded DNA, making it five or six orders denser than currently available digital media, such as flash memory. Information stored in DNA can also be read thousands of years after it was first laid down. This is exactly analogous to data storage on a computer hard drive. In this project, the DNA bases A or C were encoded with a zero and the G and T bases were encoded as a 1. In this way standard binary notation was reproduced.

Since then things have really moved on apace. For example, in 2017 researchers at Harvard Medical School published an article in the journal *Nature* describing how they were able to record complex information such as an image or a movie into bacterial genomes using DNA editing technology called CRISPRs.[9]

CRISPR is an acronym for "clustered regularly interspaced short palindromic repeats". It is actually a family of DNA sequences found within bacteria. It was discovered as an immune system of bacteria to fight against invading DNA pathogens, such as viruses. Of particular interest to the researchers was that bacteria use the CRISPR/Cas9 system to record in their DNA information about viruses they encounter. They are, in effect, writing a manual on how to protect themselves against harmful viruses for use by future generations. This is exactly what we do when we create libraries and, in more recent years, record information on computer hard drives and in other digitally readable media.

DNA is the "hard drive" in every cell of the body. The four molecules are like a sequence of data. DNA is a digital storage medium. If we can manipulate the sequence, we can also store information.

A finger of DNA (equivalent in size to a test tube) can hold approximately 1 petabyte (PB) of data, the equivalent of 1.5 million CD Rom discs. For comparison, it has been suggested that the human brain can store about 2.5 petabytes of memory data. Put another way, a PB is just over one quadrillion bytes (1,125,899,906,842,624). This means that all the present digital information in the whole world, encoded in DNA, would easily fit in the back of one SUV or estate car.

So how much "information" do you contain? Well, every cell of your body contains about a billion DNA bases arranged in a particular four-letter code. So to calculate the number of possible combinations you have to raise 4 to the power of one billion. This results in 2 billion bits contained in an area a trillionth of the volume of a matchhead.

On 22 February 2019 a paper was published in the academic journal *Science*, describing an astounding breakthrough about the information storage of DNA. The paper announced that a group of scientists had managed to create an additional four DNA bases and, in doing so, had increased the DNA alphabet available for data storage from four to eight. This new system has been called Hachimoji DNA. *Hachi* is Japanese for "eight", *moji* for "letter".[10]

These additional letters fit perfectly into DNA's double helix, and enzymes read them in the same way they read the original four. Although the four natural bases should give a large number of sequences of letters, they are actually restricted. C can only bond to G, and A can only bond to T. These strict rules help ensure that DNA strands do not clump together into a jumble.

This development effectively doubles the data storage capacity of DNA. But it has other implications too. It suggests that other forms of DNA could exist with many more bases. If they did so, what kind of life could they create?

It is important to appreciate what these discoveries mean. In effect, DNA is an information storage device, in the same way that a computer hard drive is. The amount of digital information that can be stored is vast. But there is more. Please recall Michael Harner's ayahuasca experience discussed in the last chapter. You will remember that in his "trip" Harner encountered reptilian entities who informed him that they had created life on planet Earth and now hid themselves deep within the cellular structure of all living creatures, including humankind. Now, what substance can be found deep within the human body that has a distinct reptilian (specifically snake-like) appearance? Yes, DNA. Indeed, this similarity has been noted by, among others, Jeremy Narby. So what does all this mean in relation to my Egregorial model?

We are now ready to draw this material all together.

EPILOGUE

So here we are at our destination. What have we discovered on our journey? Well, it seems that the reality we take for granted, the so-called "consensual reality" that we share with other observing consciousnesses, is simply one of a number of realities that overlap, and that these alternate realities are just as "real" as our consensual one. I make no apologies for the number of times I use the word "real" or its derivations in the above statement, because to do otherwise would fail to convey the power of this observation.

We have discussed in some detail what we actually mean when we apply the label "real" to something. We know that if we break down any material object into its component parts and continue doing this until we cannot compartmentalize it any more, we end up with virtual emptiness. We have also discovered that there is a direct relationship between the creation of the subatomic particles that provide the "solidity" of all material objects and the act of observation of those particles by a conscious observer. By the very act of observation, a subatomic particle is forced out of a wave of probabilities into a point location in space and time.

Using the ancient Gnostic terminology, we have agreed on a term for the reality created from this observer-facilitated wave function collapse: the Kenoma. You will recall that this Greek word means "emptiness", suggesting that without observers to collapse the wave function there is no "out there": things are literally empty. It seems that observers, both individually and collectively, create a seemingly three-dimensional reality out of information which is located outside the Kenoma, in a place we have agreed to call the Pleroma, Greek for "fullness".

The Pleroma is the universe "behind" this one, the greater world beyond our earthly perceptions. This dimension is denied to human beings trapped within the illusion that constitutes the sensory universe, known by philosophers as the phenomenal world – the "desert of the real", as French philosopher Jean Baudrillard has described it (in his 1981 book *Simulacra and Simulation*). (Some readers will recall my reference to the use of this phrase in a speech by the character Morpheus in the movie *The Matrix* (1999). Interestingly, early on in the movie the central character, Neo, uses a hollowed-out book to hide an illegal data disc. That book is a copy of *Simulacra and Simulation*).

But what actual evidence have we got that the phenomenal world is a mind-facilitated simulation? To appreciate how this may be the case, and why famous individuals such as technology entrepreneur Elon Musk are taking such an idea seriously, we need to go back more than 50 years to the mid-1960s.

In 1965 the co-founder of the Intel microprocessor business predicted that, owing to advances in miniaturization, the number of transistors located on a single integrated circuit board would double each year. He was wrong in this prediction: over time the year-on-year increase has dropped to a doubling every *three* years. But the levels of miniaturization have continued. When first invented, transistors were, on average, about half an inch across (1.25cm). Today's newest circuit boards contain transistors smaller than a virus. The growth of processing power is well illustrated by the fact that the navigation system in a modern standard automobile is nearly 1.8 million times more powerful than the Launch Vehicle Digital Computer that helped Neil Armstrong and his crew navigate their way to the Moon in 1969.

In 2003 Oxford University philosopher Dr Nick Bostrom published a paper in the influential *Philosophy Quarterly* suggesting that it was highly likely we are all living in a computer simulation. His logic was simple. If humanity survives self-destruction and science progresses in the way it has done over the last hundred or so years, then scientifically proven projection techniques show that the processing power available to our descendants could easily accommodate the creation of simulated universes containing simulated human beings who are programed to believe they are sentient.[1]

Bostrom's argument has one huge challenge to overcome, known as "substrate independence". This is the question of whether it can ever be possible to create sentient self-consciousness within a simulation. But this problem can be overcome quite easily if it can be shown that consciousness creates reality rather than reality creating consciousness. This was the position taken by the priest-scientist Teilhard de Chardin.

De Chardin suggested in his book *The Phenomenon of Man* that energy exists in two forms: "tangential" and "radial". The former is the energy that can be measured by scientific instruments; the latter is a form of psychic energy. Tangential energy is governed by the Second Law of Thermodynamics, whereas radial energy is not. In the early 1950s de Chardin began to believe that his tangential energy could be related to "information", and that information in itself was not subject to the Second Law.

For De Chardin, information processing, when taking place within the electrical circuits of a computer, was similar to the way in which the brain generates thought. Both are seemingly non-physical effects created by a physical process.

From this model he suggested that just as non-conscious life had spread across the planet to create a huge, interrelated biosphere, consciousness had similarly spread to cover the Earth in a non-physical form which he termed the "noosphere". The biosphere is created by tangential energy and therefore ruled by the Second Law of Thermodynamics, whereas the noosphere is created by radial energy. This was powerfully prescient, for we now know that information has created its own niche via the worldwide web and the creation of virtual realities that are rapidly becoming indistinguishable from what we believe to be "real" reality.

In his novel *Snow Crash* (1992) author Neal Stephenson takes this idea to its logical conclusion. Stephenson visualizes how the Internet may evolve in such a way that with sufficient computing power a totally immersive, virtual universe program could be created. This is a virtual universe in which the game player effectively *becomes* the avatar. The player enters a *Matrix*-like simulation that stimulates all the senses in such a way that they inhabit, to all intents and purposes, an actual reality.

Of course, this is fiction, but recent developments in computer simulations suggest that such an idea is not as strange as it seems. A central tenet of modern quantum physics is something known as "quantum chromodynamics". This describes the workings of one of the four fundamental forces of nature, the strong nuclear force. This is the force that binds quarks and gluons together to form protons and neutrons. We are now in a position to program computers to simulate how this force develops. Using the world's most powerful supercomputers, scientists have been able to simulate a tiny corner of the cosmos that is a few femtometres across. A femtometre is 10^{-15} metres. This may sound like a ridiculously small area: a quadrillionth of a metre or 0.000000000001mm. But this does nothing to undermine the point that a small area of "reality" has been fully simulated in a computer program. Indeed this fabricated reality is, to all intents and purposes, indistinguishable from the real thing. We are only restricted by computer power in this regard. Given a big enough computer containing tiny transistors, it is only a matter of time before the threshold of a few micrometres will be reached. This is large enough to simulate a human cell.

If this is the case, then it is not beyond comprehension that in a few hundred years we may have sufficient computing power to simulate a whole universe. Indeed, with this possibility in mind, could it be possible that a hugely advanced civilization has already simulated a universe – and that we exist within it? Is this not what I describe in my concept of the Kenoma? – that is, an emptiness that is filled with non-physical digital data in the same way that your computer screen, or latterly your VR headset, is filled with seemingly three-dimensional realities in which you can move about at will?

Of course, there is evidence that we already have a processor that can create at least one virtual universe: the human brain. Every millisecond your brain takes the data sent to it by your various sensory processor units and creates a model of external reality that it presents to your consciousness. Just like the simulations created by a computer, this inner model is a facsimile in exactly the same way that the virtual reality environments found in modern-day computing are facsimiles.

My idea of the Pleroma, the place where Egregorials are created, is simply the universe outside our particular "kenomic" program. In the terminology of the proponents of the simulation argument, this is known as the Metaverse.

Intriguingly, in Stephenson's novel a new form of narcotic substance, the eponymous snow crash, seems to allow the Metaverse to leak through into the "physical world". A snow crash is, in fact, what we see on a computer screen when the system crashes. Here we have a fictional recreation of the Persian Sufi concept of the Alam al-Mithal, the gateway between the Malakut (Pleroma) and Molk (Kenoma). Here is a modern-day version of Corbin's *Mundus Imaginalis* in the guise of a compelling and influential work of fiction.

I readily admit that what I am proposing is total speculation, but it is based upon a developing model of understanding of how the universe functions. Matter is not prime: consciousness is. Consciousness creates matter in the same way that a computer converts digital information into sounds and images on a computer screen or creates a seemingly three-dimensional virtual reality environment when a VR headset is attached to the computer.

My suggestion that the perceptual universe may be equivalent to a VR computer simulation is not as far-fetched as it may first appear. In an article published in July 2014, Craig Hogan, a cosmologist at Fermilab, hypothesized that our perceptual universe is like a "four-dimensional video display". He argued that if we stare deeply enough into the structure of matter, we will discover the bitmap of our holographic universe in the same way that if you look closely enough at a computer screen, you will eventually spot the individual pixels.[2] In 2013 the German GEO600 gravitational wave detector found the "pixilation" that Horgan had suggested would exist if the universe was a hologram.

In other words, there is strong reason to believe that this universe and everything in it is a super-hologram created out of digital information. If this is so, then Bostrom may be right. We are all existing in a computer game of our own lives created by our descendants.

Let us assume that Bostrom, Musk and De Chardin are correct in their assumptions. If the physical world is, in fact, created purely from non-physical digital information then the existence of non-human intelligences existing outside the program is not so far-fetched. Our Egregorials are simply sentient programs in the same way that we are sentient programs. They just exist on a different level. It may be that the code in which they are written is different. However, this does not mean that they cannot be perceived within the Pleroma: it is just a question of the perceptual abilities of the perceiver. And this is where things become quite interesting. It has long been noted that what I term the Egregorials seem to reflect the cultural, religious, scientific or philosophical beliefs of the society in which they manifest. Examples include the way in which the goddess entities of pre-Christian times became Blessed Virgin Mary visions, and the way in which UFO pilots changed from being humanoid to being bug-eyed monsters and latterly "greys". The entities perceived fulfil the expectations of the observers. This suggests that in some very real sense they are both created by, and influence, the receiving/creating consciousness. There seems to be some kind of feedback loop here.

We are at the start of an exciting period of discovery about the true nature of reality and its close relationship with consciousness. The universe is turning out to be a far more complex place than we could ever have imagined. In my opinion, humanity's experiences of Egregorials throughout history offer us a vital clues about what is really going on. And we must continue to follow these clues, wherever they may take us.

NOTES

Introduction: A Mission Statement (ppix–xxi)

1 Personal correspondence.
2 Dyal, Myron, *The Boy Nobody Wanted*, unpublished, p85.
3 Stavish, Mark, *Egregores: The Occult Entities That Watch Over Human Destiny*, Inner Traditions (2018), p.3.

Prologue: My Mother and Dr Johnson (pp1–8)

1 Hancock, Graham, *Supernatural: Meetings with the Ancient Teachers of Mankind*, Random House (2006), p49.

PART ONE: PREQUELS

Chapter 1: Prehistory (pp11–22)

1 Hancock, Graham, *Supernatural: Meetings with the Ancient Teachers of Mankind*, Random House (2006), p255.
2 Eliade, Mircea, *Shamanism: Archaic Techniques of Ecstasy*, Penguin Arkana (1989), p34.
3 Pratt, Christina, *An Encyclopedia of Shamanism*, Rosen Publishing (2007), pp29–30.
4 Halifax, Joan, *Shamanic Voices: A Survey of Visionary Narratives*, Penguin Arkana (1991), p184.

Chapter 2: Ancient Civilizations (pp23–34)

1 Black, Jeremy, and Green, Anthony, *Gods, Demons and Symbols of Ancient Mesopotamia: An Illustrated Dictionary*, University of Texas Press (1992), p34.
2 Frecska, Ede, *Inner Paths to Outer Space*, Park Street Press (2008), p239.

3 https://commons.wikimedia.org/wiki/File:Ancient
_Akkadian_Cylindrical_Seal_Depicting_Inanna_and
_Ninshubur.jpg

4 Black, Jeremy, and Green, Anthony, *Gods, Demons and Symbols
of Ancient Mesopotamia: An Illustrated Dictionary*, University of
Texas Press (1992), p34.

Chapter 3: The Middle Ages (pp35–45)

1 Lactantius, *Ira Dei*, 13, pp21–2.

PART TWO: OVERLAPPING THEMES

Chapter 4: The Secret Commonwealth (pp49–65)

1 *The Secret Commonwealth*, http://www.sacred-texts.com/neu/celt
/sce/sce04.htm#fn_2, p22.

2 Ibid., p32.

3 Sanderson, Stewart, "A Prospect of Fairyland", in *Folklore* (1964),
vol. 75, no1, p1.

4 Evans-Wentz, Walter Yeeling, *The Fairy-Faith in Celtic Countries*,
Oxford University Press (1911), p486.

5 Ibid., p26.

6 Ibid., p63.

7 Ibid., p19.

8 Cooper, Roger, "Bernard Sleigh, Artist and Craftsman 1872–1954",
Journal of the Decorative Arts Society (1997), 21, pp88–102
(https://www.jstor.org/stable/41809258).

9 http://psican.org/index.php/ufological-information/1018-ufo
-fairy-folk.

10 Ibid.

11 Ibid.

12 Hodson, Geoffrey, *Light of the Sanctuary*, Theosophical Publishers
Inc (1988), p1.

Chapter 5: The Occult (pp66–85)

1 Benjamin Woolley, *The Queen's Conjuror: The Life and Magic of
Dr Dee*, Harper Press (2001), p210.

2 Ibid., p214.

3   Peterson, Joseph H, *John Dee's Five Books of Mystery*, Weiser Books (2003), p354.

4   Ibid.

5   Dee, John, *The Diaries*, 8 and 9 May 1583, pp80–82.

6   DuQuette, Lon Milo, foreword to *The Book of Abramelin*, trans. Georg Dehn and Steven Guth, Ibis Press (2006).

7   https://www.sacred-texts.com/grim/abr/abr002.htm, p26.

8   Grant, Kenneth, *Concerning the Cult of Lam* (1987), https://www.parareligion.ch/lam-stat.htm.

9   Crowley, Aleister, *Scholarship of Thelema*, The Hermetic Library (undated), ch1, p2.

10 Caves, Tom, *Mindessence: The Polarity of Life and Death*, MWI Publishing (2010), p68.

11 Murray, Braham, *The Worst It Can Be Is A Disaster*, Methuen (2007), pp101–2.

Chapter 6: Religious Egregorials: Virgins and Angels (pp86–93)

1   Allman, Toney *Miracles*, Greenhaven Publishing (2008), p5.

2   http://www.catholic.org/mary/appartns.html.

3   Pelletier, Joseph, *The Sun Danced at Fatima*, Assumption College (1952), p123.

Chapter 7: Entities of Mind Power (pp94–101)

1   Owen, Iris, and Sparrows, Margaret, *Conjuring up Phillip*, Harper & Row (1976).

2   Cavendish, Richard, *The Black Arts,* Routledge and Kegan Paul (1967).

3   Meyer, Meghan L, Hershfield, Hal E, Waytz, Adam G, Mildner, Judith N, Tamir, Diana I, "Creative expertise is associated with transcending the here and now", Journal of Personality and Social Psychology (April 2019), vol. 116(4), pp483–94.

4   Rogo, Scott, *Minds and Motion: The Riddle of Psychokinesis*, Taplinger Publishing (1978), p197.

5   Eno, Paul F, *Turning Home: God, Ghosts and Human Destiny*, New River Press, Kindle Edition (2006), p105.

Chapter 8: Messages from Spirit and Alien Realms (pp102–113)

1 Moses, W Stainton, *Spirit Teachings*, http://meilach.com/spiritual/books/st/spcover.htm.
2 Moses, W Stainton, *More Spiritual Teaching*, London Spiritual Alliance Ltd (1898), p105.
3 Ibid.
4 Ibid., p107.
5 Ibid., p109.
6 Myers, FWH, *Proceedings of the SPR*, vol. 9 (1894), pt25.
7 Keen, Montague, Ellison, Arthur and Fontana, David, *The Scole Report*, Saturday Night Press (2011).
8 Kyle, Nick, taken from private correspondence with Anthony Peake.
9 Ibid.
10 Ibid.
11 Solomon, Grant and Jane, *The Scole Experiment*, Piatkus 2003, p138.

Chapter 9: Extraterrestrials and Abduction (pp114–131)

1 Vallee, Jacques and Aubeck, Chris, *Wonders in the Sky: Unexplained Aerial Objects from Antiquity to Modern Times*, JP Tarcher/Penguin (Putnam), (2010), p257.
2 Hancock, Graham, *Supernatural: Meetings with the Ancient Teachers of Mankind*, Random House (2006).
3 Dyal, Myron, *The Boy Nobody Wanted*, unpublished, p85.
4 Ibid., p118.
5 Eliade, Mircea, *Shamanism: Archaic Techniques of Ecstasy*, Penguin Arkana (1989), p24.
6 Ibid.
7 Evans-Wentz, Walter Yeeling, *The Fairy-Faith in Celtic Countries*, Oxford University Press (1911), p63.
8 Ibid., p487.
9 Hough, Peter and Kalman, Moyshe, *The Truth about Alien Abductions*, Blandford (1997), p11.
10 Shanon, Benny, *The Antipodes of the Mind*, Oxford University Press (2010), prelims.

11 Peake, Anthony, *The Infinite Mindfield*, Watkins (2013), pp1–2.

12 Meissl, H and Yanez, J, "Pineal Photosensitivity: A Comparison with retinal photoreception", *Acta Neurobiologiae Experimentalis* 54 (1994), pp19–21.

13 Lyh-Horng Chen, "What is the soul, but a humble pineal gland?", *New Scientist*, Dec 15–21 2007.

PART THREE: ACCESSSING THE EGREGORIAL REALM

Chapter 10: The Natural Liminals (pp135–159)

1 https://www.marquette.edu/maqom/slavonicenoch.html.

2 Adler, Shelley R, *Sleep Paralysis: night-mares, nocebos, and the mind-body connection*, Rutgers University Press (2011), p13.

3 https://www.sacred-texts.com/grim/abr/abr002.htm, p28.

4 Roney-Dougal, Serena, *The Faery Faith*, Green Magic, Kindle edition (2003), loc {??] 800.

5 Cornell-Bell, AH, Finkbeiner, SM, Cooper, MS, and Smith, SJ, "Glutamate induces calcium waves in cultured astrocytes: long-range glial signalling", *Science*, 1990, 247, pp470–73.

6 Koob, A, *The Root of Thought: Unlocking Glia: The Brain Cell That Will Help Us Sharpen Our Wits, Heal Injury, and Treat Brain Disease*, Pearson FT Press, NJ, 2009, p200.

7 Koob, A, "The Root of Thought: What Do Glial Cells Do?", *Scientific American*, 27 October 2009.

8 Plato, *The Republic*, 514a–17a.

9 Blake, William, *The Marriage of Heaven and Hell*, Dover Publications (1994), p14.

10 Mack, John E, *Passport to the Cosmos: Human Transformation and Alien Encounters*, White Crow Books (2008), p148.

11 Ibid., p154.

12 Mack, Jon E, *Abductions,* Pocket Books (1995), pp115–16.

13 Hancock, Graham, *Supernatural: Meetings with the Ancient Teachers of Mankind*, Random House (2006), p319.

14 Ring, Kenneth, *The Omega Project*, Kindle edition (2011), loc871.

15 Ibid., loc652.

16 Ibid., loc667.

17 "Aliens under my bed", *Fortean Times*, 306, October 2013, p69.

18 Lilly, John C, *The Center of the Cyclone: An Autobiography of Inner Space*, Julian Press Inc (1972), p111.

19 Mack, John E, *Passport to the Cosmos: Human Transformation and Alien Encounters*, White Crow Books (2008), p172.

20 Ibid.

21 Peake, Anthony, *The Infinite Mindfield*, Watkins (2013), p99.

Chapter 11: The Chemical Liminals (pp160–181)

1 Bicknell, Joseph, "Cognitive Phenomenology of Mind Manifestation", *Breaking Convention: Essays on Psychedelic Consciousness*, Strange Attractor Press (2013), p211.

2 Tanne, Janice Hopkins, "Humphry Osmond", *British Medical Journal*, 328 (7441) (2004), p713.

3 Fish, MS, Johnson, NM and Horning, EC, "Piptadenia Alkaloids. Indole Bases of P. peregrina (L.) Benth. and Related Species", *Journal of the American Chemical Society*, November 1955, 77 (22).

4 Sai-Halasz, A, Brunecker, G and Szára, S, "Dimethyltryptamine: a new psycho-active drug" (unpublished English translation), *Psychiatrrio et neurologia*, 135 (1958), pp285–301.

5 Szára, S, *Interview conducted by email on the discovery of DMT and speculations regarding the phenomenology of the experience*, eds AR Gallimore and DP Luke, 2014.

6 Meyer, Peter J (compiler), *340 DMT Trip Reports*, (2010), http://www.serendipity.li/dmt/340_dmt_trip_reports.htm.

7 Luke, David and Spowers, Rory (eds), *The DMT Dialogues*, Park Street Press (2018), p4.

8 Harner, M, *The Way of the Shaman*, Harper & Row (1980), p1.

9 Ibid.

10 Harner, Michael, in *Shamanism: A Reader*, Graham Harvey (ed), Psychology Press (2003), p46.

11 Narby, Jeremy, *The Cosmic Serpent*, Phoenix (1998), p7.

12 Luke, David, "Disembodied Eyes Revisited: An Investigation into the Ontology of Entheogenic Entity Encounters", *The Entheogen Review*, vol. xvi, no. 1 (2008), p2.

13 Ibid.

14 Ibid., p6.

15 Voss, Angela and Rowlandson, William (eds), *Diamonic Imagination: Uncanny Intelligence*, Cambridge Scholars Publishing (2013), p288.

16 Shanon, Benny, *The Antipodes of the Mind*, Oxford University Press (2010).

17 László, E, *Science and the Akashic Field*, Inner Traditions (2007).

18 Bose, SN, "Plancks Gesetz und Lichtquantenhypothese", *Zeitschrift für Physik* 26 (1924), p178.

19 http://www.physorg.com/news160408487.html.

20 Hirano, I, Hirai, N, "Holography in the single photon region", *Applied Optics*, 25 (1986), pp1741–2.

21 Liberles, SD, "Trace amine-associated receptors are olfactory receptors in vertebrates", *Annals of the New York Academy of Sciences*, 1170 (2009), pp168–72.

22 Strassman, R, *DMT: The Spirit Molecule: A Doctor's Revolutionary Research into the Biology of Near-Death and Mystical Experiences*, Brumby Books & Music (2001).

Chapter 12: Egregorial Science (pp182–200)

1 Tonomura, A, Endo, J, Matsuda, T and Kawasaki, T, "Demonstration of single-electron buildup of an interference pattern", *American Journal of Physics*, 57 (1989), p117.

2 Wheeler, John A, *Science and Ultimate Reality: Quantum Theory, Cosmology and Complexity*, Cambridge University Press (2004), p184.

3 Ibid., 209.

4 Wheeler, John A, "Information, Physics, Quantum: The Search for Links", *Proceedings of the 3rd International Symposium on the Foundations of Quantum Mechanics*, Tokyo (1989), p356.

5 Wheeler, John A, quoted in Davies, PCW and Brown, JR, *The Ghost in the Atom*, Cambridge University Press (1986), p66.

6 Wheeler, John A, "Information, Physics, Quantum: The Search for Links", *Proceedings of the 3rd International Symposium on the Foundations of Quantum Mechanics*, Tokyo (1989), p364.

7 Hoyle, Fred, *The Intelligent Universe*, Michael Joseph Ltd (1983), p19.

8 Davies, Paul, *The Demon in the Machine*, Penguin (2019), p24.

9   Shipman, SL, Nivala, J, Macklis, JD and Church, GM,
    "CRISPR–Cas encoding of a digital movie into the genomes
    of a population of living bacteria", *Nature*, 547 (July 2017),
    pp345–9.
10 Hoshika, Shuichi et al., "Hachimoji DNA and RNA: A genetic
    system with eight building blocks", *Science*, vol. 363, issue 6429
    (2019), pp884–7.

Epilogue (pp201–207)

1   Bostrom, N, "Are You Living in a Computer Simulation?",
    Philosophical Quarterly, vol. 53, no. 211 (2003), pp243–55.
2   Horgan, Craig, *Now Broadcasting in Planck Definition*,
    arXiv:1307.2283 [quant-ph] FERMILAB-PUB-13-685-A
    (2014).

INDEX

Guardian Angel, 78, 138
Guardians, The, 104

Hachimoji DNA, 199, 216
Hades, 51, 114
Hallowell, Michael J, 139, 140,
    141, 147
Hallowell, Mike, 96
Hancock, Graham, 3, 12, 13,
    14, 117, 125, 149, 209, 213
Hard Problem of Science, 173
hares, 142
Harleian Manuscripts, 75
Harner, Michael, 165, 166, 214
Harvard Medical School, 147,
    198
Hausa civilisation, 169
hayyot, 38
Heathrow Airport, 61, 64
heavenly light, 89
Hebrew Bible, 27
Hebrews, 27
Hedin, Sven Anders, 123
Heisenberg Uncertainty
    Principle, 174
hekhal, 38
Helios, 27
Hermetic Order of the Golden
    Dawn, 76
higgs boson, 183
Hinduism, 65
Hirai, Atsushi, 175
Hirano, Isuki, 175
Hodson, Geoffrey, 63, 64, 65,
    210
Hohningstadt, Arnaud, 84, 85
Holograms, 175
Holy Cross Cemetery, 118

Holy Guardian Angel, 67
Holy Qur'an, 40
Horos, The, 7
Horus, 78
Hoshangabad, 12, 149
Hough, Peter, 122
Hoyle, Fred, 196, 197, 215
human-fish hybrids, 12
humanoid, 12, 13, 23
huskerah, 156
Huxley, Aldous, 56
hybrids, 27
Hyde, Douglas, 53
hypnagogia, 105, 138
Hypnagogic Light Experience,
    126
hypnagogic realm, 43
hypnagogic state, 42

Iblis, 43
ice-cream vendor, 125
Igigi, 24
ikuyas, 157, 158
illuder, 74
imagination muscles, 98
Imperator, 104, 105, 106, 107
Imperator and Rector, 102,
    108
implants, 125
imposter spirits, 106
Inanna, 26, 34, 210
indolethylamine
    N-methyltransferase, 179
Indonesia, 11
Inglewood, xvi
In-Sane, 178
insectoid, 161
Invizikids, 140, 141, 180

WATKINS
1893

The story of Watkins began in 1893, when scholar of esotericism John Watkins founded our bookshop, inspired by the lament of his friend and teacher Madame Blavatsky that there was nowhere in London to buy books on mysticism, occultism or metaphysics. That moment marked the birth of Watkins, soon to become the publisher of many of the leading lights of spiritual literature, including Carl Jung, Rudolf Steiner, Alice Bailey and Chögyam Trungpa.

Today, the passion at Watkins Publishing for vigorous questioning is still resolute. Our stimulating and groundbreaking list ranges from ancient traditions and complementary medicine to the latest ideas about personal development, holistic wellbeing and consciousness exploration. We remain at the cutting edge, committed to publishing books that change lives.

DISCOVER MORE AT:
www.watkinspublishing.com

Read our blog

Watch and listen to
our authors in action

Sign up to
our mailing list

We celebrate conscious, passionate, wise and happy living.
Be part of that community by visiting

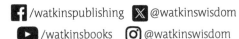

 /watkinspublishing   @watkinswisdom
 /watkinsbooks   @watkinswisdom